The Globalisation Issue

ISSUES

Volume 98

Editor

Craig Donnellan

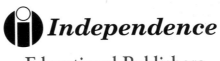
Independence

Educational Publishers
Cambridge

First published by Independence
PO Box 295
Cambridge CB1 3XP
England

British Library Cataloguing in Publication Data
The Globalisation Issue – (Issues Series)
I. Donnellan, Craig II. Series
337

ISBN 1 86168 312 X

Printed in Great Britain
MWL Print Group Ltd

Typeset by
Claire Boyd

Cover
The illustration on the front cover is by
Simon Kneebone.

CONTENTS

Overview

Chapter One: The Debate

Introduction

The Globalisation Issue is the ninety-eighth volume in the **Issues** series. The aim of this series is to offer up-to-date information about important issues in our world.

The Globalisation Issue looks at the impact of globalisation on world trade.

The information comes from a wide variety of sources and includes:
Government reports and statistics
Newspaper reports and features
Magazine articles and surveys
Website material
Literature from lobby groups
and charitable organisations.

It is hoped that, as you read about the many aspects of the issues explored in this book, you will critically evaluate the information presented. It is important that you decide whether you are being presented with facts or opinions. Does the writer give a biased or an unbiased report? If an opinion is being expressed, do you agree with the writer?

The Globalisation Issue offers a useful starting-point for those who need convenient access to information about the many issues involved. However, it is only a starting-point. At the back of the book is a list of organisations which you may want to contact for further information.

*****

Globalisation

Information from the World Bank

What is it?

Globalisation is an inevitable phenomenon in human history that's been bringing the world closer through the exchange of goods and products, information, knowledge and culture. But over the last few decades, the pace of this global integration has become much faster and dramatic because of unprecedented advancements in technology, communications, science, transport and industry.

While globalisation is a catalyst for and a consequence of human progress, it is also a messy process that requires adjustment and creates significant challenges and problems.

Why should I care?

Globalisation has sparked one of the most highly charged debates of the past decade.

When people criticise the effects of globalisation, they generally refer to economic integration. Economic integration occurs when countries lower barriers such as import tariffs and open their economies up to investment and trade with the rest of the world. These critics complain that inequalities in the current global trading system hurt developing countries at the expense of developed countries.

Supporters of globalisation say countries – like China, Vietnam, India and Uganda – that have opened up to the world economy have significantly reduced poverty.

Critics argue that the process has exploited people in developing countries, caused massive disruptions and produced few benefits.

But for all countries to be able to reap the benefits of globalisation, the international community must continue working to reduce distortions in international trade (cutting agricultural subsidies and trade barriers) that favour developed countries and to create a more fair system.

Globalisation is an inevitable phenomenon in human history that's been bringing the world closer

---

Some countries have profited from globalisation

- India: Cut its poverty rate in half in the past two decades.
- China: Reform led to the largest poverty reduction in history. The number of rural poor fell from 250 million in 1978 to 34 million in 1999.
- Vietnam: Surveys of the country's poorest households show 98 per cent of people improved their living conditions in the 1990s. The government conducted a household survey at the beginning of reforms and went back six years later to the same households and found impressive reductions in poverty. People had more food to eat and children were attending secondary school. Trade liberalisation was one factor among many that contributed to Vietnam's success.
- Uganda: Poverty fell 40 per cent during the 1990s and school enrolments doubled.

But others have not

- Many countries in Africa have failed to share in the gains of globalisation. Their exports have

- remained confined to a narrow range of primary commodities.
- Some experts suggest poor policies and infrastructure, weak institutions and corrupt governance have marginalised some countries.
- Other experts believe that geo-graphical and climatic disadvantage have locked some countries out of global growth. For example, land-locked countries may find it hard to compete in global manufacturing and service markets.

Over the last few years, there have been protests about the effects of globalisation in the United States and Europe. But in a lot of developing countries there is very strong support for different aspects of integration – especially trade and direct investment, according to a recent survey conducted by the Pew Center. In Sub-Saharan Africa, 75% of households said they thought it was a good thing that multinational corporations were investing in their countries.

History of globalisation

The most recent wave of globalisation, which started in 1980, was spurred by a combination of advances in transport and communications technologies and by large developing countries who sought foreign investment by opening up to international trade.

This is actually the third wave of a phenomenon that started back in 1870.

The first wave lasted from 1870 to the start of World War I. It was stimulated by advances in transport and reductions in trade barriers. The level of exports to world income doubled to 8 per cent as international trade boomed.

It sparked massive migration as people sought better jobs. About 10 per cent of the world's population moved to new countries. Sixty million people migrated from Europe to North America and other parts of the New World. The same thing happened in densely populated China and India where people moved to less densely populated countries like Sri Lanka, Burma, Thailand, the Philippines and Vietnam.

The end of the First World War ushered in an era of protectionism. Trade barriers such as tariffs were erected. World economic growth stagnated and exports as a percentage of world income fell back to the 1870 level.

Following World War II, a second wave of globalisation emerged, lasting from about 1950 to 1980. It focused on integration between developed countries as Europe, North America and Japan restored trade relations through a series of multilateral trade liberalisations.

During this period there was a surge in the economies of the countries in the Organisation for Co-Operation and Development that participated in this trading boom. But developing countries were largely isolated from this wave of integration, unable to trade beyond primary commodity exports.

- The above information is from the World Bank Group's website for students which can be found at youthink.worldbank.org

© The World Bank Group

Crack the code

A beginner's guide to globalisation

We all play a role in the great globalisation game. The best way to make full use of our power as citizens and consumers is by getting a grip of the different terms involved. This global glossary will get you started.

Capitalism

Capitalism is an economic system and ideology based around the idea of people trading on a market, owning private property and accumulating capital to invest in financial or industrial enterprises. Most people in a capitalist system work for private

employers, providing goods or services that are sold for profit. The state employs few people, owns no enterprises and puts few regulations on the economy.

Anti-capitalism

Anti-capitalism is a very broad term which shot into the media spotlight during the 1999 WTO summit in Seattle, where a range of people and organisations demonstrated against how the world's international economic system works. The term can cover any challenge to capitalism as the best or only way to organise the world.

Liberalisation

Liberalisation is a process of reducing the government's involvement in a country's economy, based on the idea that private businesses can run things more efficiently. It normally involves deregulation (removing government regulation and restrictions), privatisation (sale of state-owned enterprises to the private sector) and opening up economies (removing trade barriers – see Free trade).

Structural adjustment

Structural adjustment is a set of policy changes countries have to make in order to receive loans through the IMF and World Bank. It often involves liberalisation of the economy. Structural adjustment is intended to help countries become more economically efficient so they can easily repay their loans, but it has been strongly criticised for creating unemployment, and making health and education too expensive for many people.

Free trade

Free trade means governments have to treat local and foreign producers the same, for example by not creating barriers against importing goods, services or people from other countries, or giving national businesses and farmers an advantage over foreign firms by offering them financial support. In practice, truly free trade has never existed, and reducing trade barriers is always subject to intense political negotiation between countries of unequal power.

Ethical trade

Ethical trade involves companies finding ways to buy their products from suppliers who provide good working conditions, and respect the environment and human rights.

Fair trade

Fair trade encourages small-scale producers to play a stronger role in managing their relationship with buyers, guaranteeing them a fair financial return for their work.

World Trade Organisation (WTO)

The World Trade Organisation (WTO) was created in 1994 to liberalise world trade through international agreements. Based in Geneva, the WTO has 140 member countries, some of which have much more power than others (see The Quad). For instance, Japan has 25

delegates while Malawi cannot afford to keep any staff in Geneva.

The International Monetary Fund (IMF)

The International Monetary Fund (IMF) was set up in 1944 along with the World Bank to maintain a stable international trading system. It monitors countries' economies, and gives out loans to help the international economic system function more smoothly. The IMF can impose conditions on countries wishing to borrow money (see Structural adjustment). All borrowers must pay back the loan within a specified time and are charged interest.

The World Bank

World Bank is the main organisation providing financial help for development. Originally established to help Europe recover after the Second World War, it has also provided loans for structural adjustment in developing countries since 1980. By 1990, developing countries owed the World Bank US$89 billion in debt. Smaller regional development banks in Africa, Asia and Latin America work in the same way, but with fewer resources.

The Quad

The Quad is a name given to the four most economically and politically powerful groups of countries in world trade: the European Union, the United States, Japan and Canada. They don't always agree on policy, but when their interests coincide

they become a very dominant group in forums like the WTO.

Debt

Debt is money a government owes to either another country, private creditors, or international agencies like the IMF or World Bank.

Aid

Aid means transferring resources from industrial to developing countries in many different ways: one country can support a specific project in another; an international organisation can decide to spend money on supporting a country's economy; specialised staff or equipment can provide technical assistance, or loans are given with a special repayment rate.

Multi-National Corporations (MNCs)

Multi-National Corporations (MNCs) are companies that operate in many different countries beyond the one where they are registered. An MNC sells its products and services globally, and often has offices and staff in several countries. Its products are often made step by step across several continents. The world has a rapidly growing number of MNCs, which are becoming increasingly powerful.

■ The above information is an extract from *RightAngle*, the magazine produced by Save the Children. For more information see their website at www.savethechildren.org

© *Save the Children*

The rough guide to globalisation

A CAFOD briefing

'Is globalisation only to benefit the powerful and the financiers, speculators, investors, and traders? Does it offer nothing to men, women, and children ravaged by the violence of poverty?'
Nelson Mandela, Davos World Economic Forum, February 1999.

Summits of world leaders are dogged by anti-globalisation protests; media scandals regularly expose the wrongdoings of powerful corporations in poor countries. Globalisation is in danger of becoming a swearword. Yet in Doha, the capital city of Qatar, the world's governments (most of them of poor countries) in 2001 launched a round of global trade talks that will speed up global integration. The British Government swears that globalisation is a force for good, offering new hope to the world's poor. Yet millions of poor people and grassroots groups in the developing world vehemently disagree. To shed some light on a heated debate, this briefing explains what globalisation is, its impact on the poor countries of the world, and what needs to change. CAFOD has been charting the impact of globalisation on development for many years, and is currently running a four-year campaign on trade and food security (2001-5).

What drives globalisation?

Globalisation describes the process whereby individuals, groups, companies and countries become increasingly interconnected. This interconnectedness takes place in several arenas:

Global logo inc.

The inexorable rise of giant transnational corporations (TNCs) lies at the heart of globalisation. Brand names, from Nike to Coca-Cola, have become some of the most widely recognised images on the planet. Of

the world's top 200 economic players in 2001, 56 are countries and 144 are corporations. General Motors, Wal-Mart, Exxon Mobil, and Daimler Chrysler all have revenues greater than the combined economic output (GDP) of the 48 least developed countries.

With economic power has come political clout. World leaders scramble for audiences with Bill Gates (Microsoft) and John T. Chambers (Cisco). Corporate lobbyists are enormously influential (though often invisible) in drawing up the laws governing global trade and investment. Supporters of globalisation argue that TNCs bring jobs and new technology to developing countries, while critics worry that their growing political might is undermining national governments and allowing corporations to run the global economy to suit themselves and their shareholders.

The world in your supermarket

Rich and poor countries alike have bought into the globalisation message – that you can export your way out of under-development. From 1980 to 2001, world trade in goods (not services) tripled from £1 trillion to

nearly £4 trillion. Poor countries have concentrated on clothes, footwear, electronics, and food – a trip down the aisle of your local supermarket has become a tour of the Third World, with asparagus from Peru, prawns from Bangladesh, and mangetout from Zambia. China has become the world's largest exporter of clothing, toys, electronics, and shoes. Trade can create jobs and wealth in poor countries, but the regular media exposés of appalling working conditions in Third World farms and factories have led to increasing concern over the social and environmental conditions under which the goods are produced.

Globalfuture.com

The accelerating pace of innovation in information technology (IT) is driving globalisation. The cost of a three-minute phone call from New York to London fell from $245 in 1930, to $3 in 1990, to about 35 cents in 1999 (1990 prices). Using 24-hour email, companies can split up their assembly lines between countries on different sides of the globe, sending designs and orders down the phone line and shifting components from one country to another to minimise costs. IT can cut costs and create a global village, but has awakened fears of a growing 'digital divide' between the haves and have-nots. Thailand has more cellular phones than the whole of Africa.

One Disney McWorld

The doubling of tourism over the last 15 years, and increased international migration, have meant greater cultural contact between countries and peoples. The spread of information and corporate branding has generated something akin to a single global culture, especially among the teenagers of the MTV generation. Those hyping globalisation believe this will lead to greater international understanding. Others fear that the global cultural tapestry could be replaced by bland corporate imagery and the platitudes of 'Just do it' branding. Priests in Latin America have told CAFOD they have been asked to baptise children from poor families with names like Rangerover, Thissideup and Iloveny (think about it).

$2 trillion a day

Capital flows, increasingly disconnected from any real trade or investment, have grown enormously in the last 15 years. They now run at about $2 trillion a day (that's 12 zeros), moving around in the Alice-in-Wonderland world of derivatives, futures, and currency trading. The capital crossing the world's borders in three days exceeds a whole year's global trade. Globalisation's supporters argue that capital flows can provide much-needed investment, for example via Third World stock markets, and can deter governments from following unwise economic policies which endanger 'market confidence'. However, such massive capital flows can easily overwhelm even large economies (as Norman Lamont found out in 1992). Since 1997, capital surges have caused severe social and economic crises in Thailand, Korea, Indonesia, Russia and Argentina. The World Bank has found that these crises tend to hit the poor hardest, while subsequent recoveries benefit the better off, ratcheting up inequality.

Globalisation and the poor

In the age of the internet, 1.3 billion people worldwide have to live on less than 70 pence a day, and 800 million people do not have enough to eat. Globalisation may not be wholly, or even mainly, to blame for these facts, but neither has it had much impact on ending them.

One reason that globalisation has failed to benefit the poor is inequality. In a highly unequal society, the poor receive less benefit from economic growth. Rising inequality, both between and within nations, has been one of the most alarming features of recent decades. In 1960, the income ratio of the poorest 20 per cent to the richest 20 per cent of the world's population was 1:30. Today it is 1:74. The assets of the world's top three billionaires come to more than the combined economies of all the least developed countries and their 600 million people.

One problem is unequal access to technology – one CAFOD partner in Peru talks of *los desenchufados*, the 'unplugged ones' among the Andean farmers, who are unable to benefit from new technology and fall ever further behind their richer neighbours. Inequality is also driven by financial instability and unfair terms of trade between rich and poor nations. If the political will is there, improvements can be made in all these areas. A fall in inequality would benefit rich and poor alike – as the World Bank points out, countries with lower inequality grow faster and consume more imports.

Globalisation has affected the working lives of the poor. Although jobs may be created, CAFOD has seen in many countries how competition between countries can lead to a 'race to the bottom': each country competes for foreign investment by offering lower wages, fewer unions or rights at work, and more tax breaks for corporations, all of which reduce the potential benefits of investment to the host country and the workforce. The 'anxious society' of temporary contracts and vanishing job security is not just a British problem, but a global one. In the UK the cost of clothes and footwear has fallen by a third in the last 15 years, in part because labour is getting ever cheaper. A Nike quilted jacket costs £100 in a London shop, but only 51p of that goes to the Bangladeshi women who make it. CAFOD has found garment workers in Indonesia earning 57p for a 10-hour day.

In the countryside, globalisation has spelt disaster for many poor farmers when developing countries have suddenly opened their economies to imports, often as part of the 'structural adjustment programmes' required by the IMF and the World Bank in return for loans and debt relief. Unable to get access to credit or modern technology, they have been expected to compete with northern agribusiness, which enjoys huge subsidies from its governments. The average European cow receives support of $2.20 a day, more than the income of half the world's people,

enabling Europe to dump artificially cheap milk powder on countries such as Jamaica and Brazil, with devastating consequences for local dairy farmers. In Mexico, prices received by maize farmers halved after the North American Free Trade Agreement opened the borders to subsidised US maize.

What needs to change?

The debate should not be about whether we are pro- or anti-globalisation. Some form of globalisation is a given. But globalisation is not like the weather, beyond any government or individual's control. As Secretary of State for International Development Clare Short has pointed out, the rules of globalisation have been designed by people and can be changed by people. There is nothing inevitable about the rules that established the WTO, the North American Free Trade Agreement, or, for that matter, the EU. Given sufficient political will, it is quite possible to regulate corporations, stabilise international financial flows, and ensure that the poor benefit fully from the potential offered by increased trade and investment. CAFOD believes that the logic of globalisation needs to change – trade and investment should be recognised as a means to an end, and that end is human development and the eradication of world poverty. To do this, some key concerns must be addressed:

Reform of the institutions of globalisation

In an unplanned, ad hoc way, globalisation has come to be administered by several key institutions. Best known are the World Trade Organisation, the World Bank, and the International Monetary Fund, but there are many others. Most of them have been criticised for the same failings – a lack of transparency and accountability, an ideological bias in favour of deregulation and the reduction of governments' role in managing the economy, and the disproportionate influence exerted on them by a few powerful governments. If globalisation is to work for the poor, these institutions must be reformed.

Ending northern double standards

The EU and US preach free trade, but often fail to practise it. The EU slaps taxes on Third World exports and dumps its subsidised produce in developing country markets, destroying local livelihoods. Battalions of US lawyers earn a living by bending the rules to keep out Third World imports, claiming risks to health or dumping. When new WTO rules are drawn up, they usually reflect the balance of power within the organisation, benefiting the richer countries, for example by permitting the kinds of subsidies used in the North, but banning those used in the South. As long as this 'you liberalise, we subsidise' attitude continues, globalisation is likely to look to many Third World governments and citizens more like an exercise in northern self-interest than a real opportunity for progress.

Kicking away the ladder

The rules that govern globalisation include the idea of 'national treatment' – that a government should treat foreign investors and companies at least as well as domestic companies. Yet all the successful countries discriminated in this way when they were at earlier stages in their development. Some economists argue that they are using global trade rules to 'kick away the ladder' from developing countries wishing to follow their example.

Undermining sovereign governments

Globalisation can undercut national sovereignty by drastically reducing a government's options. Some say this is a good thing, preventing national governments from pursuing 'unsound' economic policies. But it can equally well prevent them pursuing policies that benefit the poor, for example by putting food security and small farmers first, rather than

---

CAFOD believes that the logic of globalisation needs to change

---

opening all their markets to cheap foreign imports. Trade rules must not prevent developing countries from pursuing the right policies for development.

Corporate responsibility

Following the 'privatisation of power' in the hands of large corporations in recent years, companies must take proper responsibility for their social and environmental impacts. Regulation can curb the worst corporate excesses and ensure companies are required to report publicly about their social and environmental impact, but corporate cultures and management must also change if they are to be effective.

Can globalisation be reformed?

CAFOD believes there is no choice. The debacle at the WTO ministerial meeting in Seattle in November 1999 showed that the status quo is not an option. For the well-being of all the world's peoples, developing countries and their citizens must be given a greater voice in, and see greater benefits from, the evolving global system. That will require political will from decision makers, North and South, but also active involvement by citizens and non-governmental organisations.

Both in its work with partners overseas, and with its supporters in England and Wales, CAFOD is committed to this process. Through the Ethical Trading Initiative, it works with corporations keen to improve wages and conditions in their overseas suppliers. In its public campaigning, it has drawn attention to the need for reform of global trade rules and turning the spotlight onto the devastating impact of the Common Agricultural Policy. All these efforts are essential if the forces of globalisation are to be harnessed in the service of the greatest crusade of our times, the drive to end the scandal of global poverty.

■ This guide was written by Duncan Green of CAFOD's Public Policy Unit. For more information visit their website which can be found at www.cafod.org.uk

© CAFOD

The IMF and World Bank

The facts

Origins

The World Bank and the IMF were formed at the Bretton Woods Conference in 1944, called to establish a new global economic order at the end of World War Two. The influential economist John Maynard Keynes proposed a stable, fair world economy in which trade surpluses were automatically recycled to finance trade deficits. Instead the US pushed for a system based on the dollar and on the free movement of capital. The IMF and the Bank were designed to smooth out the wrinkles of currency and capital shortages.

The IMF was intended to oversee currency values and act as a kind of 'credit union' from which national governments could draw short-term loans when they were in balance-of-payment difficulties. It has evolved into an international judge of countries' macroeconomic policies, offering loans conditional upon the adoption of a raft of free-market measures.

The IBRD (International Bank for Reconstruction and Development) is commonly known as the World Bank. It was designed to loan money to rebuild war-torn and 'underdeveloped' nations. Most of its money comes from bonds sold on the international markets; most of its money has tended to go into big infrastructure projects such as dams, power plants and roads.

There are four other members of the World Bank Group:

- The IFC (International Finance Corporation) was founded in 1956 to invest in or make loans to private companies operating in borrowing countries. It must make a profit and therefore can never benefit the poorest directly. 85% of its money goes into 15 countries that could attract investment on the international markets anyway.
- The IDA (International Development Association) was set up in 1960 to make long-term low-

interest loans to the poorest countries. This headed off attempts by newly independent Third World countries to establish an independent funding agency within the UN.

- The ICSID (International Center for the Settlement of Investment Disputes) has since 1966 served as a tribunal settling disputes between governments and corporations.
- The MIGA (Multilateral Guarantee Investment Agency) appeared in 1988. It provides political risk insurance to corporations undertaking projects in the developing world.[1]

Power and control

Voting power in both the IMF and the World Bank is broadly based on economic power. The 30 countries of the OECD (Organisation for Economic Co-operation and Development – broadly the rich world plus a select few) control almost two-thirds of the votes in both the IMF (63.55%) and the World Bank (61.58%). The G8 countries alone control almost half the votes (48.18% of the IMF, 45.71% of the Bank).

Practical power in both the Fund and the Bank rests with their Boards of Directors. There are 24 Directors on each Board. The 8 countries in the chart have their own Director on both Boards. Other member countries are divided into blocs, with one nation 'representing' them on

the Board. Just 2 Directors represent sub-Saharan Africa on the IMF Board, for example, wielding 4.43% of votes between them.

The US has by far the most powerful Director, with a 17.14% vote in the Fund and 16.39% in the Bank. The US has stated that it will not allow its voting power in the IMF to drop below 15%, which gives it a veto over all key decisions.[2]

Adjustment: enemy of growth

The IMF and the World Bank claim that the structural adjustment programmes they have imposed on developing countries are in the service of long-term economic growth. In practice four decades of global experience tell a different story. As adjustment lending has ballooned, so economic growth has gone into reverse, the two graph lines acting as a mirror image.[3]

Poverty incorporated
45% of the $25 billion that the World Bank lends each year is dispensed directly to Western transnational corporations.[4]

Institutionalised failure
In 2000, the Joint Economic Committee of the US Congress found a failure rate of 55-60% for all World Bank-sponsored projects. In Africa, the failure rate reached 73%.[5]

The debt disgrace

The poorest nations of the world are drowning in debt. Current commitments to debt relief such as the much hyped Highly Indebted Poor Countries (HIPC) initiative, have achieved little.

Net negative transfer
In 1999, the HIPC countries repaid $1,680 million more than they received in the form of new loans.

For every dollar in grant aid to developing countries, more than 13 comes back in debt repayments.[5]

The IMF and World Bank – the statistics

Voting rights in the IMF, % of total votes, 2003[2]

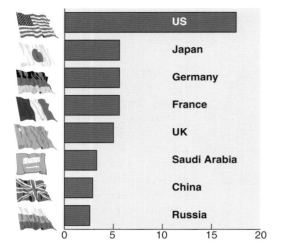

US	
Japan	
Germany	
France	
UK	
Saudi Arabia	
China	
Russia	

(scale: 0, 5, 10, 15, 20)

How growth in developing countries has fallen as adjustment lending has risen[3]

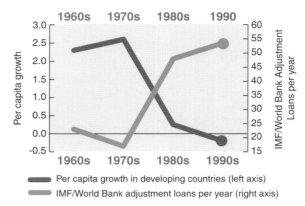

- ▬ Per capita growth in developing countries (left axis)
- ▬ IMF/World Bank adjustment loans per year (right axis)

Aggregate % voting power in the IMF, 2003[2]

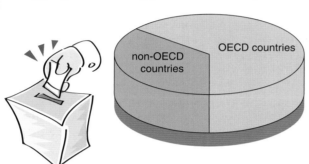

non-OECD countries — OECD countries

Enhanced HIPC Total Debt owed to World Bank/ International Monetary Fund and Multilateral Development Banks (2000-03)[5]

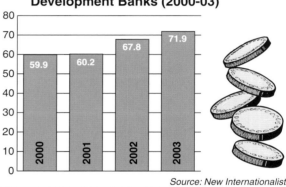

2000	2001	2002	2003
59.9	60.2	67.8	71.9

Source: New Internationalist

Hiccoughs in the HIPC

Between 1996 and 1999 the overall amount of debt-servicing payments from the HIPC increased by 25% (from $8,860 million in 1996 to $11,440 million in 1999).[5]

Between 1990 and 1996 HIPC debt increased by 30%. In 1996, the G7, the IMF and the World Bank announced a cancellation of up to 80% but in practice, far from diminishing, the debt continued its upward curve and climbed a further 4.7% in 5 years.[5]

Cancel the debt!

The IMF, World Bank and the regional development banks (African Development Bank, Asian Development Bank, Inter-American Development Bank) hold a wealth of resources, approximately $633 billion in effective capital and $60 billion in reserves and provisions for loan losses.[6]

According to the US Government's International Financial Institution Advisory Commission, these banks can easily marshal internal resources for total debt cancellation for HIPC countries as it represents just 5% of their effective capital.[6]

All monetary values are expressed in US dollars.

References

1 Information from www.worldbank.org and *Empty Promises*, The 50 Years Is Enough Network, Washington, July 2003.

2 www.imf.org www.worldbank.org

3 William Easterly, *The Elusive Quest for Growth*, MIT Press, Cambridge, Massachusetts, 2002, p102.

4 The Corner House, *Exporting Corruption: Privatization, Multi-nationals and Bribery*, June 2000.

5 World Bank, 'Global Development Finance', 2001-03 and IMF 'World Economic Outlook' 1996-03. Joint BIS-IMF-OECD-World Bank statistics on external debt. www1.oecd.org/dac/debt/

6 United States Government, 'International Financial Institution Advisory Commission (Meltzer Commission) Final Report', March 2000. www.house.gov/jec/imf/meltzer.htm

■ Reprinted with kind permission of the *New Internationalist*, Copyright New Internationalist www.newint.org

© *New Internationalist*

Trade

Information from the World Bank

What is trade?

Trade allows people to buy goods and services that are not produced in their own countries. In addition, the money countries receive from exports helps determine how much they can afford to spend on imports and how much they can borrow from abroad.

Exports

Goods and services a country sells to another country.

Imports

Goods and services a country gets from another country to sell domestically.

Trade can stimulate a country's development and economic growth. This helps create new jobs, raise living standards and gives people an opportunity to take charge of their lives.

People in all countries – developed and developing alike – can benefit from international trade that is free of barriers, such as tariffs, quotas and government subsidies.

- As consumers: people could choose from more, better made and less expensive products
- As producers: people could sell their goods in more markets

International trade is a much more effective way to reduce poverty than outright aid because trade can help a country become self-sufficient, instead of relying on foreign aid. There are, however, many inequalities in international trade that work against poor countries.

International trade is regulated through a set of rules that the world's governments have created over the years. In general, poor countries don't have access to markets in developed countries because of trade barriers and agricultural subsidies. Trade barriers make it difficult for poor countries to sell their products abroad and improve living conditions back home.

Although free trade benefits all people, governments sometimes try to protect their products and markets from external products by providing subsidies to local producers, or erecting barriers, such as tariffs and quotas. This practice is known as protectionism.

Subsidies

Governments giving money to local producers to make the cost of their goods artificially low.

Tariffs

A list of taxes placed by a government on imported or exported goods.

Quotas

The amount or the number of goods that can be imported or exported.

Protectionism

Protecting domestic producers by impeding or limiting the importation of foreign goods and services. This is done through tariffs or quotas.

When producers receive extra money (subsidies) from their government, they can afford to sell their goods at a much lower price than those goods are really worth on the market. This is a particularly big problem in agriculture.

Why should I care?

By placing tariffs and import quotas on foreign products, governments try to make those products more expensive for domestic consumers. This is to encourage consumers to continue buying domestically produced goods, which will continue to be less expensive, though – in reality – they may be more expensive to produce than a similarly made foreign product.

Since economies of poor countries aren't well developed or diversified, they often produce only a handful of products that can be sold competitively abroad. It becomes difficult for them to find ways to develop and improve the lives of their people when trade barriers limit or prohibit where or when they can sell these products abroad.

The consequences of these trade inequalities are at the core of the criticism about globalisation. Many international organisations, from the World Bank to non-governmental organisations (NGOs), work to change the world trading system to make it more fair and equal for all countries, including the poorest ones.

World Trade Organization (WTO)

Most countries in the world are members of the World Trade Organization (WTO). WTO members meet every few years to discuss how to liberalise international trade.

Liberalising trade would remove all tariffs and quotas, and allow goods and services to sell only for what they are really worth. This would help poor countries enter new markets and sell their goods.

If WTO ministers could agree to slash tariffs in agriculture and manufacturing, the resulting changes in trade could lift more than 140 million people out of poverty.

While WTO works to update and liberalise the international trade rules, it is difficult to negotiate new rules that would meet every country's expectations and concerns.

In addition to being a member of WTO, countries that trade a lot with one another often create

> *International trade is regulated through a set of rules that the world's governments have created over the years*

separate rules to regulate the flow of goods and services between them. They give each other's products preferential terms than to products from other countries that aren't part of these agreements.

Bilateral trade agreements: when two countries create a separate agreement that regulates the terms of trade between them.

Regional trade agreements: when several countries enter into special arrangements to trade among themselves under more favourable conditions. Mercosur (Mercado Comun del Cono Sur – Southern Cone Common Market – between Argentina, Brazil, Paraguay and Uruguay) and NAFTA (North American Free Trade Agreement, between Canada, the United States, and Mexico) are examples of such regional trade agreements.

■ The above information is from the World Bank Group's website for students which can be found at youthink.worldbank.org

© *The World Bank Group*

Free trade

The facts

Free trade is an old idea that's taken on new life over the past decade – January 2004 marked the tenth anniversary of the North American Free Trade Agreement (NAFTA). Free trade is part of a broad process of trade liberalisation being pursued by Western governments as well as the WTO, the World Bank and the IMF.

Ebbs and flows
The vast majority of the value of world merchandise trade – about 75% – is accounted for by manufactured goods, mostly transport machinery and electronic equipment. Minerals and agriculture, the staples of the developing world, make up just 22% of merchandise trade.

■ With the exception of East Asia and Central America, developing country exports have not increased significantly over the past 40 years.

■ The share of South America, Central and Eastern Europe and Africa in total world exports was lower in 2002 than in 1960.

■ While world exports grew at an annual rate of 6% in the 1980s, exports from the poorest countries grew at a rate of just 2% a year.

■ The value of world exports of services jumped by more than 300% between 1980 and 2002 – from $400 billion to about $1,600 billion.

■ Rich countries dominate the service trade, both exports and imports, accounting for 70.6% of world imports and 73.2% of exports in 2002.

■ From 1980 to 2002 developing countries' share of global service exports increased while imports dropped. Asia accounted for most of the export growth (from 10% in 1980 to 17% in 2002) while both exports and imports in Latin America and Africa plummeted.

Swimming upstream
It's hard to get rich by trading when the value of your exports is falling in relation to your imports. Declining terms of trade are a major barrier to poor countries trading their way out of poverty. The boom-and-bust cycle of commodity prices stymies development and impedes planning.[5]

■ From 1997 to 2001 commodities lost more than half their purchasing power compared to manufactured goods, meaning poor countries had to export twice as much to purchase the same amount of imports. Cotton prices fell 47% from 1998 to 2001 and coffee fell by 69%.

■ Between 1980 and 1998, 19 of the world's 25 poorest countries experienced declining terms of trade. In both Nigeria and Uganda terms of trade fell by 70%.

■ If terms of trade for non-oil exporting countries in Africa had not declined over the past 20 years the current level of per capita income would have been as much as 50% higher after adjusting for inflation.[6]

Subsidies and protectionism
The rules of international trade are rigged to benefit the rich. Poor countries are told to lower their tariffs, exploit their 'comparative advantage' and trade their way to wealth. At the same time rich countries refuse to dismantle existing trade barriers and give massive subsidies to their own export industries.

■ Rich countries spend $1 billion a day on domestic agricultural subsidies – more than 6 times what they spend on overseas aid every year. Since 1997 these subsidies have increased by 25%.[7]

■ US protectionism alone may cost the poor countries $50 billion a year in lost agricultural exports.[8]

■ For key agricultural exports like sugar, rice and dairy products the major economic powers maintain tariffs of 350-900%. In contrast the World Bank and IMF have imposed steep tariff cuts on developing countries in return for 'structural adjustment' loans.[7]

■ The European Union pays tomato farmers a minimum price higher than the world price while processors are also subsidised. As a result EU tomatoes 'dumped' into West Africa now make up 80% of the local supply and have nearly destroyed the domestic industry.

■ Under the FTA agreement with the US, Central American countries are required to eliminate tariffs on rice, beans, corn and dairy products while the US refuses to lower its own subsidies on these products. This will threaten the livelihoods of nearly 5 million small and medium farmers throughout the region.[9]

Commodity blues

Decades after the demise of colonialism, much of the Majority World is still dependent on a handful of primary exports.

- In 1998-2000, 70 poor countries received more than half their export earnings from just three commodities.[3]

Trade *über alles*

Free trade gives power to corporations and investors in return for the promise of economic growth. By adopting a one-size-fits-all model, governments sacrifice sovereignty and control of their own development priorities.

In Mexico after 10 years of NAFTA

Exports increased 300% from 1993 to 2002 to $161 million. But . . .

- Annual GDP growth has been less than 1%.
- More than half of manufactured exports have been from the oil industry or from low-wage maquiladora assembly plants along the US border.
- Of the 6 biggest export firms, 5 are foreign-owned and account for more than 20% of total exports.[10]

FTAA timeline

Miami, Florida, 1994 President George H Bush launches negotiations on a hemispheric free trade deal at the first Summit of the Americas. The goal of the Free Trade Area of the Americas or FTAA is 'free trade from the Arctic to Tierra del Fuego'.

Santiago, Chile, 1998

Thirty-four nations set up FTAA Trade Negotiations Committee with nine working groups: agriculture, services, investment, dispute settlement, intellectual property rights, competition policy, government procurement, market access and subsidies/anti-dumping.

Quebec City, Canada, April 2001

FTAA draft text completed at the Summit of the Americas amidst mass public demonstrations.

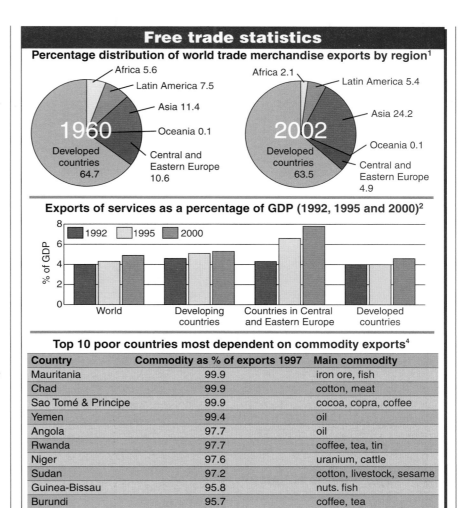

Free trade statistics

Percentage distribution of world trade merchandise exports by region[1]

1960:
Africa 5.6
Latin America 7.5
Asia 11.4
Oceania 0.1
Central and Eastern Europe 10.6
Developed countries 64.7

2002:
Africa 2.1
Latin America 5.4
Asia 24.2
Oceania 0.1
Central and Eastern Europe 4.9
Developed countries 63.5

Exports of services as a percentage of GDP (1992, 1995 and 2000)[2]

(bar chart, % of GDP, legend: 1992, 1995, 2000; categories: World, Developing countries, Countries in Central and Eastern Europe, Developed countries)

Top 10 poor countries most dependent on commodity exports[4]

Country	Commodity as % of exports 1997	Main commodity
Mauritania	99.9	iron ore, fish
Chad	99.9	cotton, meat
Sao Tomé & Principe	99.9	cocoa, copra, coffee
Yemen	99.4	oil
Angola	97.7	oil
Rwanda	97.7	coffee, tea, tin
Niger	97.6	uranium, cattle
Sudan	97.2	cotton, livestock, sesame
Guinea-Bissau	95.8	nuts. fish
Burundi	95.7	coffee, tea

Source: New Internationalist

Quito, Ecuador, March 2002

Draft text updated and re-released at the 7th FTAA Trade Ministerial.

Miami, Florida, November 2003

At the 8th FTAA Trade Ministerial, spirited public protests and strong opposition by Brazil, Venezuela, Argentina and Ecuador derail the talks. Further meetings scheduled for September 2004. Talks grind to a halt.

Washington, December 2004

Final text to be ready for heads of state, with country-by-country ratification during 2005 and implementation by December 2005.

References

1 *Development and Globalization: Facts and Figures 2004*, p51 UNCTAD.
2 *Development and Globalization: Facts and Figures 2004*, p61 UNCTAD.
3 *Trade and Development Board, Background Notes*, 10 October, 2003, UNCTAD.
4 *European Fair Trade Association Newsletter*, Vol 1, No 5, July 2001, p9.
5 'Free market freefall: declining agricultural commodity prices and the market access myth', Gerald Greenfield, *Focus on the Global South*, July 2004.
6 *Trade and Development Board, Background Notes*, 10 October 2003, UNCTAD.
7 *Making Global Trade Work for People*, p8 Kamal Malhotra, UNDP/ Earthscan, 2003.
8 *The myth of free trade as a development model*, Laura Carlsen, www.americaspolicy.org
9 *Rights and Development*, Washington Office on Latin America, March 2004, p2.
10 *Lessons from NAFTA: the high cost of free trade*, www.policyalternatives.ca

Globalisation

Is it the perfect way forward for world trade, or the evil mechanism of inequality? Make your own mind up.

What is globalisation?

Globalisation is the rapid integration of trade and culture between the world's nations. With a more open market, goods – and by association, cash – can now travel across the globe much more freely. This greater global trade has been able to happen for these reasons:

- Governments have changed laws that in the past restricted economic trade.
- New technologies have enabled faster communication.
- Travel and transport costs have reduced dramatically.
- Foreign (western) companies have looked abroad for investment.

International bodies such as the World Trade Organisation and the European Union were partly created to help reduce the barriers to trade and investment and allow the global marketplace to blossom.

For many, globalisation is a good thing:

- Better standard of living. Increased international trade has made us wealthier and allowed us to lead more diverse lifestyles. Globalisation has provided greater choice on the high street, rising living standards and a growth in international travel.
- Bringing the world together. By promoting global growth, supporters believe it could even reduce poverty and increase equality worldwide. They say it has promoted information exchange, led to a greater understanding of other cultures and brought us together. All of which educates workers across the globe on how they should be treated and encourages people to stand up for their rights. Life expectancy in the developing world has risen from 46 to 64 in the last 40 years.

> *With a more open market, goods – and by association, cash – can now travel across the globe much more freely*

For others, it's not such a good thing

Environmentalists, anti-poverty campaigners, trade unionists and anti-capitalist groups see the growth of global companies raising more problems than it solves. They believe the West's gain has been at the expense of developing countries whose share of the global income has dropped from 2.3% to 1.4% in the last decade. Others fear that by becoming a global community we are losing our cultures, traditions and differences that make individuals special and add colour to the world, in favour of a vacuous Hollywood-stamped world.

Transnational corporations (TNCs)

TNCs base their operations in more than one country so they can avoid laws and regulations that would otherwise tie them down. They manufacture goods where labour is cheapest, base their operations where taxes are low and sell the goods where the price is highest. They have been criticised for putting shareholders ahead of their workers, their

customers and the environment. 500 TNCs now control two-thirds of world trade, and 90% of these are based in the developed world placing profits back in the pockets of the richest. The world's three richest men have combined assets equal to the output of the world's 48 poorest countries and their 600m people.

The race to the bottom

Developing countries are desperate to attract foreign investment and they believe will create jobs and alleviate poverty. Global institutions like the International Monetary Fund (IMF) advise them to reduce barriers to trade and attract investors by keeping labour costs down. Countries then end up competing with each other to drive down wages and conditions, in what is known as

the 'race to the bottom'. Winners of the race are unlikely to get their dream at the end of it. Employees often face harsh working conditions, long hours and a pittance of a wage.

While the developing world is struggling to attract trade, there is also a backlash against western workers as TNCs move their production plants abroad where wages will cost them so much less.

What can be done to lessen the negative effects of globalisation?

Forming trade unions will get the workers' voices heard, and try to start to get companies to put people before profit. There is also a need for the world to adhere to a basic set of workers' rights and universal rules for trading and working in the global market. In 1998 the International Labour Organisation, a protector of the basic rights of people at work, set out its 'Fundamental Workers' Rights', and while they haven't solved the problem yet, they are trying hard to enforce them globally.

■ The above information is from TheSite's website which can be found at www.thesite.org

© TheSite.org

The effects of globalisation

Information from Oxfam GB

In our globalised world, the lives of people in rich and poor countries are closely linked. However, the systems that operate, through trade rules for instance, mean that in the globalisation game there are both winners and losers.

Growing inequalities

■ The population of the world is 6 billion
■ 1.2 billion people live on the equivalent of 65 pence a day
■ 2.8 billion people live on the equivalent of £1.30 a day

For many, the 1980s and 1990s – the years of increasing globalisation – were also decades of increasing wealth. The world's total economy grew, benefiting from new technology, liberalisation and growth of trade. However, at the same time, the gap between rich and poor was also growing wider, both within and between countries. Former World Bank chief economist Joseph Stiglitz argues that globalisation left millions of people worse off in 2000 than they were in 1990. Even though more wealth is being generated by trade

Oxfam

than previously, there are still 1.2 billion people who live on the equivalent of less than 65 pence a day and 2.8 billion who live on less than £1.30.

The figure of 65 pence a day is used as a guideline to measure and compare poverty levels around the world. It is generally agreed by the international community that those living on the equivalent of this amount or less each day are unlikely to be able to provide themselves and their families with a standard of living considered acceptable for a healthy and fulfilled life. However, this does not mean that all those living on 65 pence a day or less consider themselves to be poor, as the concept of poverty varies widely across countries and communities.

Changing patterns of trade

The price received by coffee growers for their produce has decreased by 70 per cent since 1997.

One of the key features of globalisation has been the dramatic growth in international trade. Between 1981 and 2001, the volume of world trade grew twice as fast as world GDP. Countries in the South have played an active role in this process by exporting more, and their dependence on exports has grown rapidly. This has meant that such countries have become much more vulnerable when the price of their exports on world markets has fallen. Many depend on primary commodities for their share of exports and income. For example, coffee plays an essential role in the livelihoods of poor people in approximately 50 countries in the developing world. It is estimated that about 20 million households produce the crop, which is often the main – sometimes the only – source of cash income. International coffee prices have decreased by 70 per cent since 1997.

During the 1990s a growing number of countries with large populations turned to the export of manufactured goods as a way of generating employment and income. In countries such as Bangladesh, 1.7 million people, mainly women, have been drawn into Export Processing Zones (EPZs), making garments. EPZs offer inducements to foreign companies to set up manufacturing. Workers' wages are exceptionally low by international standards but they still earn twice as much as agricultural labourers.

Well-managed trade has the potential to reduce poverty. If developing countries increased their share of world exports by five per cent, this would generate $350 billion – seven times as much as they receive in aid. In fact, the poorest countries currently face the world's most restrictive trade barriers.

Changes in employment conditions

Foreign investment by TNCs has the potential to create a large number of jobs – estimates, though difficult, put the figure at between 17 and 26 million people. Through their sheer size and domination of global markets, TNCs also strongly influence employment conditions.

Some people argue that TNCs should use their influence to improve wages and conditions in factories. TNCs respond by saying that their wages are often higher than local rates of pay and offer employment opportunities to large numbers of people.

The environment

There is growing concern that globalisation is damaging the planet. Our environment continues to deteriorate, and many renewable resources such as fresh water, forests, plants and animal species are being exhausted beyond their natural recovery level. This is most striking in the fishing sector where more than 40 per cent of fish stocks are now at risk because the fish are being caught more quickly than they can reproduce themselves. This situation directly affects the one billion people who depend on fish as their main source of protein.

The consumption patterns of richer countries are a prime source of environmental destruction and lead to global warming. On a per capita basis, emissions of carbon dioxide are almost 20 times higher in the USA than in India. The richer countries of the world, with 14 per cent of the world's population, produce an estimated 60 per cent of greenhouse gas emissions. Transport alone produces 21 per cent of current carbon dioxide emissions and its share is growing rapidly.

> *The main accusation by the anti-globalisation movement is that poor countries are denied an opportunity to benefit on an equal footing with rich ones*

It would seem that globalisation is leading to a greater awareness that our environment is shared. Yet the future health of the Earth is still unclear. The failure of the Kyoto Protocol – which aimed to reduce the level of greenhouse gas emissions – underlines the challenges that the global community faces.

Debates on globalisation

Recent years have been marked by an increasingly heated debate over globalisation.

Lately, anti-globalisation campaigners have organised alternative gatherings whenever an economic summit takes place. When world leaders were attending the World Economic Summit in Davos, Switzerland, in 2003, 100,000 people

gathered in Porto Alegre, Brazil, for the World Social Forum. The emphasis was on peaceful discussion, the sharing of views, and the building of alliances. The main accusation by the anti-globalisation movement is that poor countries are denied an opportunity to benefit on an equal footing with rich ones. In the other camp, enthusiasts for globalisation counter that economic growth is a good thing. According to them, trade leads to poverty reduction.

The debate over whether globalisation is inherently good or bad may not be helpful. Most people would agree that globalisation is here to stay. However, it is also a process managed by people and governed by rules such as those that dictate international trading patterns. These rules can be changed, and many people believe that, if they are, globalisation can be made to work to the benefit of everyone, including the poorest.

Glossary

Gross Domestic Product (GDP)
The total value of new goods and services produced in a given year within a country.

Export Processing Zones (EPZs)
An area designed to encourage foreign companies to set up manufacturing in a country by offering inducements such as a tax-free period or exemption from labour laws. They contain factories producing for transnational companies and have been established throughout the South.

Kyoto Protocol
Agreed in Japan in 1997, the Kyoto Protocol, part of the International Climate Change Convention, stipulated targets for developed countries to cut their greenhouse gas emissions. These targets continue to be the subject of dispute.

■ The above information is from Oxfam's Cool Planet website www.oxfam.org.uk/coolplanet with the permission of Oxfam GB, 274 Banbury Road, Oxford, OX2 7DZ www.oxfam.org.uk Oxfam GB does not necessarily endorse any text or activities that accompany materials.
© *Oxfam GB*

Globalisation: a dirty word?

Globalisation: the exploitation by the affluent West of the Third World poor? The pillage by greedy multinationals of the labour and natural resources of people who have insufficient clout to negotiate a better deal? Or the only hope for a better life for millions in developing countries?

Oxfam and many other development organisations believe trade can play a vital part in poverty reduction when the right conditions are met. Trade can equally be hugely damaging for poor people if it undermines their livelihoods by destroying their markets or ruining their environment.

In the foreword to the Oxfam report on trade, globalisation and the fight against poverty, *Rigged Rules and Double Standards*, Oxfam's honorary president and Nobel Economics Laureate, Amartya Sen, writes:

'Global interaction, rather than insulated isolation, has been the basis of economic progress in the world. Trade . . . has helped to break the dominance of rampant poverty and the pervasiveness of "nasty, brutish and short" lives that characterised the world.'

But the report identifies a crucial paradox of global trading – that at the same time as being a source of unprecedented wealth, millions of the world's poorest people are being left behind.

'World trade has the potential to act as a powerful motor for the reduction of poverty, as well as for economic growth, but that potential is being lost. The problem is not that international trade is inherently opposed to the needs and interests of the poor, but that the rules that govern it are rigged in favour of the rich.'

The report analyses the rules governing world trade and puts forward Oxfam's policy goals for correcting the balance between the extremes of western prosperity and of Third World poverty, in launching its 'Make Trade Fair' campaign.

The Co-op fully supports Oxfam's position that the right path is not one of 'no trade', but of 'fair trade'.

Although long committed to a responsible retailing policy in our relationships with customers and suppliers, the Co-op does not believe in product boycotts.

'World trade has the potential to act as a powerful motor for the reduction of poverty, as well as for economic growth, but that potential is being lost'

Supermarket brands are particularly anonymous and are often supplied by major companies. The Co-op is determined to make this relationship more transparent. The choice of supplier is crucial, if retailer and customer want to make a real difference to the livelihood of that supplier.

Products like bananas and mangoes, fruit juices, tea, coffee, cocoa and many more are sourced entirely or in part from growers in the Third World.

Conditions vary depending on country, region and produce, but there are five common characteristics. Growers tend to be:

- subject to massive fluctuations in the price they receive for their produce, caused by the speculation of commodity traders in New York and London
- dominated by local or regional wholesalers, who are often profiteering middlemen
- disparate, small scale and remote – many living on subsistence levels, with little or no money to invest in improvements
- dependent on crops that are labour intensive and use low-technology means of planting, crop protection and harvesting
- exposed to climatic conditions that drastically affect quantity and quality of crop.

The combination of these factors makes growers weak and vulnerable. When prices fall, growers are faced with uncomfortable choices: they want to send their children to school but they cannot afford the books or uniforms. They need the support of all members of the family, but they cannot afford

medicine to keep their family well.

Food self-sufficiency becomes the first goal of survival, which can lead to the neglect of the cash crop, especially where the price they get for selling it is less than the cost of producing it. If things get worse, even basic expenditure on food will need to be cut, weakening growers' capacity for productive work and leaving them vulnerable to health problems.

As a retailer we can make a difference through our choice of supplier and the conditions of supply.

And we can provide moral support for producers, in the knowledge that they are being supported by a major retailer.

- We can offer a decent and – equally as important – stable price for their produce
- We can shorten the supply chain, by cutting out exploitative middlemen and dealing more directly
- We can reduce fragmentation by encouraging the development of co-operatives, bringing econ-

omies of scale, mutual support and more negotiating muscle.

Perhaps the best example of this is the Fairtrade initiative, on which the Co-op has a unique track record, and which it has supported more than any other retailer since its inception.

- The above information is from Co-operative Group (CWS) Limited's website which can be found at www.co-op.co.uk

© Co-operative Group (CWS) Limited

Questions young people ask about globalisation

Information from the International Youth Parliament (IYP)

Is economic growth always a good thing? Is continuous growth of the economy and the current process of globalisation the only means to prosperity?

Growth (or expansion of the economy) may not always be a good thing. The current form of inequitable and unsustainable economic growth we are experiencing is damaging our natural environment, because it relies on the consumption of the world's finite supply of natural resources.

While these resources are consumed for the benefit of growth, the environmental impact on the planet is often disregarded. The idea of 'sustainable development' is less destructive: it proposes a system that meets the needs of today, without destroying the ability of future generations to meet their needs.

The increased prosperity of globalisation goes hand-in-hand with mass poverty, and the widening of the gap between rich and poor. But well-managed and equitable growth has the potential to lift people out of poverty.

Economic growth must be accompanied by social, environmental and labour policies to be truly beneficial. Stable agricultural prices, open markets for developed nations,

environmental regulations, protection of developing countries' markets, investment in public health and education, and corporate regulation are essential parts of equitable and sustainable economic growth.

The belief that the economy must grow is closely linked with the means of measuring this growth. The most common measure is Gross Domestic Product (GDP), which is the sum of all that is produced in a given economy. This measure of growth is not a measure of well-being or quality of life.

Some limitations of GDP include 'negative' costs, such as environmental disasters which are added into the value of GDP. GDP doesn't include work-at-home or the cash economy, or things that can't be measured; and GDP does not show us how wealth is distributed.

Alternative measures of economic growth do exist. They reflect

different aspects of the economy that can be measured and managed independently, and sustainably. The Genuine Progress Indicator (GPI) uses 20 measures ignored in GDP, such as resource depletion and the loss of leisure time. This measure suggests a decline in these factors since the 1970s.

According to the GDP, young people are entering a better world than their parents. According to the GPI, the opposite is true.

It may also be noted that increased economic growth and prosperity does not necessarily create happier citizens. Despite higher levels of personal wealth, life expectancy, economic growth and development of societal infrastructure, many industrialised nations are recording increasing levels of stress, depression and relationship breakdown.

If free trade provides jobs, better living conditions, access to the world and reduced levels of poverty, is trade the answer to global prosperity?

While trade can be used in the fight against global poverty, the current rigged rules and double standards of global trade are generating incredible wealth for some, and unsustainable poverty for others.

It is widely assumed that an increase in free trade is always a good thing. While trade itself can be beneficial, the proposition that trade is always good depends on what's being traded, the power relationship in the trade, for whom the trade is beneficial, and the rules which govern it.

The World Trade Organization (WTO) is pushing for a free trade agenda, free from any subsidies or tariffs. However, under the current system, there is a question of whether trade is actually free in both directions. Is the trade free for developing countries as well as wealthy countries? Many poorer farmers cannot compete against subsidised, mass-produced foodstuffs and are consequently falling further into poverty.

Oxfam's Make Trade Fair Campaign states that rich countries spend US$1 billion every day on agricultural subsidies. Excess goods resulting from these subsidies are introduced into world markets, undermining the livelihoods of millions of smallholder farmers in developing countries.

When developing countries export to the markets of rich countries, they face tariff barriers four times higher than those encountered by rich countries when they export. Those barriers cost them US$100 billion a year: twice as much as they receive in aid.

What impact has the push for 'free trade' had on developing countries? From their point of view, the costs are usually overlooked. For example, trading rules don't cover labour standards. Some powerful transnational companies (TNCs) have been left free to engage in investment and employment practices that contribute to poverty and insecurity. These practices are only regulated by weak voluntary guidelines. In many countries, success in export markets is partly built on the exploitation of young women and girls.

International Monetary Fund (IMF) and World Bank loan conditions have forced developing countries into trade, and into opening their markets. While this is done to service their debt, it is often at the expense of adequately feeding and

sheltering their young people. Additionally, as developing nations export commodities, the market becomes increasingly competitive.

As a result, agricultural prices fall, making it difficult for many developing countries to expand their export earnings. Coffee prices, for example, have fallen by 50% since 1999 to a 30-year low, costing exporters in developing countries US$5 billion in lost foreign-exchange earnings in 5 years.[1] Oxfam argues that the creation of a new international commodities institution to promote price stability and end over-supply would go a long way to making trade more fair.[1]

Does the collapse of other systems of exchange – such as communism – prove that a free market is the only way to run an economy?

Like all systems of exchange, free market economics is an ideology, not a given. Globalisation has been promoted as a victory for democracy and the free market economy, and the fairest and most efficient mechanism for allocating resources. In practice, globalisation has operated to the exclusion of many, to concentrate economic power in the hands of a few.

Using unlimited expansion of trade and foreign investment as measures of economic progress doesn't necessarily result in healthy communities. Productive assets are often owned by foreign corporations, education and health systems become operated on a profit, user-pays basis, and local productivity by local populations for local populations is lost.

When the World Bank and IMF place demands on developing countries to rapidly open up their markets, the consequences for poor communities and those living in poverty are damaging. Additionally, the argument that the free market always works is not valid in developing nations, which don't yet have a solid infrastructure in education, health and basic social services.

Before opening markets up, developing nations need time to strengthen anti-corruption measures and protect vulnerable industries, as well as develop effective taxation systems and agricultural land management reform policies.

When overseas companies invest in a country, does that foreign investment provide high quality jobs, technology transfer and greater efficiency?

Many countries are attempting to make their economies more attractive to foreign investment. Foreign investment can bring benefits to an economy, but we need to ask who benefits and who loses in the equation. We also need to ask what the cost is to the community and environment.

'Becoming competitive' is used as an argument for many public policy settings: reducing company taxes; reducing government expenditure; balancing budgets; reducing safety nets; lowering environmental protection standards and watering down rights. The creation of a more 'flexible workforce' is often accomplished by lowering standards of employment, and increasing numbers of casual workers.

The WTO has argued that environmental standards, quarantine standards, public ownership and national security considerations are all 'trade barriers'.

Foreign investment can have positive impacts but often takes over business previously run by a country's citizens, can negatively impact on a country and its communities.

Damaging consequences also arise from downsizing, threatening to relocate that business to another country (in turn, placing further pressure on the host government), losing control of decisions affecting the local economy, and governments acting as tax havens to attract and subsidise investment of questionable value.

When considering foreign investment, short and long-term considerations must be understood. Thorough assessments must question whether the investment provides the new technology required by the host country, whether the project invests in a better future and what the profit motive is. Do these risks outweigh the potential instability and loss of control following the investment? If there is a profit, will it stay in the local economy?

Foreign investment which is invested for quick profit has the potential to destabilise countries. As capital markets become more mobile, they become more unpredictable. Domestic markets become more vulnerable to capital 'flight' (i.e. when capital is pulled quickly out of a country) when economic changes occur, or expectations of a country's future decline.

Will globalisation alleviate global poverty? Will wealth trickle-down to the people and will everyone benefit from the increased wealth generation?

The argument of the 'trickle-down effect' or 'trickle-down economics' is widely used to promote the current form of corporate globalisation. The argument implies that through the current form of globalisation, wealth, knowledge sharing, technology transfer and economies of scale will be shared and benefit all.

Through the implementation of fair rules of trade and other public policy settings, it is possible for globalisation to reduce widespread poverty. Through the internet, globalisation can provide information on appropriate small-scale technologies and micro credit, and allow the faces and voices of impoverished people to be seen, and heard.

However, the 'trickle-down effect' is working in reverse. Poverty and inequality remain entrenched worldwide. The significant majority of humanity is now born in developing nations, where nearly 1.3 billion people do not have access to safe drinking water, 840 million people are malnourished and one in seven children have no school to go to.

Half of humanity – three billion people – survive on less than US$2 a day. A child born in Australia will have a lifetime income 74 times that of a child born in the developing world. Forty years ago, this income gap stood at 30 to 1. One hundred years ago, it was 11 to 1.[2] In the past decade, the world's richest countries have increased their wealth by 30% and yet, overseas aid has declined by over US$12 billion.[3]

An alternative to the 'trickle-down effect' is the 'bubble up' approach. This approach empowers the underprivileged to initiate change, by making available the resources for change; through micro credit and small-scale appropriate technology, for example. This sort of development protects vulnerable communities, and starts by meeting immediate needs with small-scale, local and culturally appropriate initiatives.

Is globalisation inevitable? Is there anything we can do?

Many young people feel disempowered by globalisation. But there are positive, effective actions that can be taken. For example, two powerful globalisation processes failed because of concerted opposition: The attempt to launch a new round of tariff reductions at the WTO in 1999 received a significant set-back, and the proposed Multilateral Agreement on Investment (MAI) was stopped.

Things change. Look at the demise of South African apartheid; independence for the East Timorese from Indonesia, and debt relief programmes for the world's poorest nations.

The internet has provided our global community the enhanced capacity to communicate. In turn, that has provided an unsurpassed opportunity for ordinary citizens to become involved with the increasing number of human rights, environmental organisations and development non-governmental organisations (NGOs) acting as 'globalisation watchdogs'.

By demanding human rights and freedoms, democratised world governing bodies, sustainable development, fair trade and an equitable international financial system, real and sustainable change can be effected.

References

1 Oxfam International, Make Trade Fair: www.maketradefair.com
2 Oxfam Community Aid Abroad, 'The Globalisation Challenge', 2001
3 Ibid

■ Oxfam International Youth Parliament brings together a network of young leaders (Action Partners) working for positive, sustainable and equitable change within their own communities. To support Action Partners in their work for change, the OIYP Programme provides integrated project support (grants, online training and mentoring), ongoing strategic support and capacity building as well as access to learning and development through our research, learning and impact programmes. Find out more at www.iyp.oxfam.org

© *Oxfam International Youth Parliament*

British workers count the cost of globalisation

The spectre of tens of thousands of job losses haunts workers' unions in the US and UK, as more and more developing countries develop their service sector industries with a range of skills and savings. Panos Features gauges the reaction of British unions and considers the way forward for governments of wealthy countries. By Alex Whiting

Until recently, words like 'call centres' and 'outsourcing' in Britain stayed firmly in the business pages of newspapers, read mostly by entrepreneurs looking for the next big trend in buck-saving.

Now they are making headlines and grabbing the public's attention, as one household name after another announces its decision to move jobs overseas. Globalisation, it seems, is making its presence felt. And some don't like it.

The Communication Workers' Union – one of the largest telecommunications and financial services unions – launched a high-profile tour across the country with a giant pink inflatable elephant, campaigning against what it called the 'UK job stampede' to developing countries, where wages and other costs are dramatically lower.

'Over 200,000 office-based jobs throughout the UK are at risk in just about every sector, but especially in call centres, banking and communications,' says Geannie Drake, deputy general secretary of CWU.

The fear is understandable. In the last decade call centres have created much-needed work in British regions where manufacturing jobs were lost in the 1980s. The average wage in a call centre is £12-15,000 ($19-23,500) compared with the per capita income of $24,160. Still, the 6,000 call centres in Britain employ nearly half a million people – 1.7% of the working population.

> ### 'Over 200,000 office-based jobs throughout the UK are at risk in just about every sector, but especially in call centres, banking and communications'

Worryingly (for British unions) a recent report by Mitial International, analysts of the call centre industry, predicts a sharp drop in jobs – partly as a result of competition from cheaper destinations such as India. The report says a third of Britain's larger call centres will close by 2005, triggering about 90,000 job losses.

'Our main fear is that communities in this country could be devastated by this short-term cost-cutting and at the moment no one is taking this seriously,' says Drake.

Communities most affected are in northern England and Scotland. Typical is the city of Newcastle, 440 kilometres north of London, whose economy took a nosedive after its steel, mining and shipbuilding industries shut down in the 1980s. Things worsened when the textiles industry outsourced jobs to Asia in the 1990s.

Call centres, set up in the mid-1990s, provided welcome relief, and now employ some 27,000 people in the region.

Dai Davies, director of communications at Unifi, a union for the financial and insurance sector, is concerned about what will happen if jobs do leave these areas: 'There won't be anything to replace them. There's nothing there.'

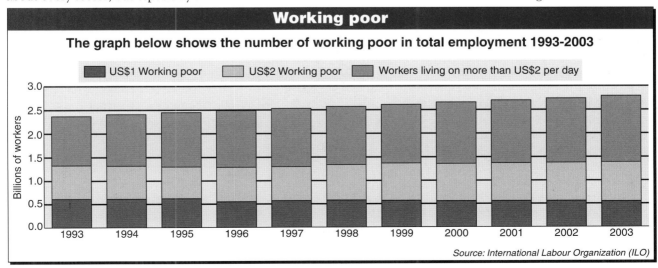

Working poor

The graph below shows the number of working poor in total employment 1993-2003

Legend: ■ US$1 Working poor ▨ US$2 Working poor ▨ Workers living on more than US$2 per day

(Y-axis: Billions of workers, 0.0 to 3.0; X-axis: years 1993–2003)

Source: International Labour Organization (ILO)

British Telecom, Britain's largest telecommunications company, is one of the latest to announce outsourcing plans. The company says it will move 2,200 jobs to the southern Indian city of Bangalore by the end of 2004. Indian staff will be paid a dollar an hour compared with nearly $10 in Britain, according to CWU.

Although BT have promised to keep all jobs, in practice many offered redeployment in other parts of Britain are likely to take voluntary redundancy instead, say unions and call centre industry analysts. Now unions are pressing for companies like BT who derive their profits from British customers to be 'socially responsible' – meaning they must support the domestic economy by employing British workers.

While outsourcing itself is not new (textiles were outsourced to Asia as early as the 1970s, manufacturing jobs in the 1980s and IT in the 1990s), the shifting of call centres and other business processes – such as administrative work and data analysis – began booming eight years ago when the multinational General Electric moved thousands of jobs from America to India. GE now has 11,000 Indian employees, mostly agents in call centres, and a core of about 400 who analyse credit card data and market trends.

India is driving the current outsourcing market, followed closely by China, South Africa, Mexico, Philippines and Ghana. According to McKinsey consultants, 203 of the Fortune 1000 list of the world's top companies outsource to India. By 2005, they estimate, business process outsourcing will be worth $235.4 billion, and India's share of this will be 10%.

The bad news for developing countries that want a larger share of the globalisation pie is that the trend seems to be causing a rush toward protectionism in the West.

The American states of Maryland, New Jersey, Washington and Pennsylvania are either considering or have already proposed legislation to ban outsourcing government contracts abroad.

In Britain, independent information technology consultants have urged the government to make it harder for Indian IT consultants to operate here. And the parliament's trade and industry committee is launching an enquiry into the loss of call centres and IT jobs overseas.

In June, India's Information Technology Secretary, Rajiv Ratna Shah, responded to the potential backlash by warning Western companies that if they limit outsourcing they will suffer in the long run. 'The stark reality of the cost advantage makes it profitable, and if they do not realise it, [firms resisting it] will cease to exist,' he said. 'It is a choice of losing some jobs, or losing all the jobs.'

India is driving the current outsourcing market, followed closely by China, South Africa, Mexico, Philippines and Ghana

---

The government agrees. 'It [outsourcing] is good for British business, and in the long term benefits the British economy,' says a Trade and Industry department spokesperson, while admitting it will cause unemployment in the short-term.

The union protests do not convince many entrepreneurs either. Ab Banerjee, chief executive of London-based financial media specialist Raw Communications, which is about to outsource its software development work to India, says: 'I think it's a huge opportunity for the UK, particularly in the pan-

European context, because outsourcing is being driven by the Indian market, and India is largely English-speaking. There are big opportunities for UK companies to stride ahead [of European rivals].'

Researchers predict outsourcing is set to increase dramatically in the near future. American analysts Forrester Research say that 3.3 million American white-collar jobs could shift to developing countries by 2015.

And British analysts at Deloitte Consulting say falling share prices and increasing competition are 'creating a "burning platform" for all financial institutions to embrace offshoring as a way of remaining competitive'.

'The reality for many companies is that while they relocate offshore for cost, they stay for quality. Indeed many companies – both financial and non-financial – discover that not only is the cost reduced for many business processes, but the efficiency and effectiveness often improves significantly.'

Dr Henry Overman, at the Centre for Economic Performance in the London School of Economics, says that while this trend is good for the British economy, it does create difficulties in the labour market, particularly for those with few skills.

'I think a worrying aspect of it is everything we understand about globalisation and liberalisation of trade says if people with lower skills want jobs, it's going to be difficult to pay them.' He says there seems to be a widening income gap between the skilled and unskilled in the West. 'But this has been going on for 20-30 years, predominantly dictated by technological changes, not outsourcing.'

One possible solution that the British government, unions and academics all propose is to retrain jobless workers in order to move them higher up the 'value chain'. 'We're a rich society, we can afford to invest in getting people skilled and that's what we should be doing,' says Overman.

■ Alex Whiting is a British journalist working for Panos Features.
© *Panos Features*

What's wrong with world trade?

Information from People & Planet

Far and away the most important globalisation issue is international trade. Worth around US$7 trillion each year, trade dominates the international agendas of most countries. Put simply trade is the everyday activity of buying and selling goods and services – something that we're all involved in. International trade could be a massive help to poor countries, enabling them to sell what they make and buy what they need. But today the global trade system is only working for the rich.

Global trade rules are keeping the poor locked in poverty

- The world's poorest countries have seen their share of world trade decline by more than 40% since 1980.
- The poorest 20% of the world's population now receives less than 1% of global wealth – and the gap is widening.
- The poorest 10% of the world's population now participates in less than 0.5% of world's trade.

International trade is governed by a set of rules agreed by governments and overseen by the World Trade Organisation (WTO). Of course international trade does need rules – but they should be rules that prevent the rich and powerful nations from using their economic power unfairly against poor and vulnerable nations. However the current WTO trade rules are unjust and don't work for the poor.

people & planet
student action on world poverty and the environment

Although trade rules are made by countries, it is companies that do the trading. And the companies of the richest countries have been able to make most of the gains from international trade, often at the expense of developing countries.

Global trade rules put big business first

'The WTO services agreement is first and foremost an instrument for the benefit of business.'
European Commission
WTO website

- About two-thirds of world trade is accounted for by 500 large corporations.
- Three companies account for 83% of world trade in cocoa, six companies control 85% of world grain trade, and three companies account for around 80% of world banana sales.

The unjust trade rules created by WTO agreements are often the result of close relationships between negotiators from the most powerful countries in the WTO and business lobby groups. These relationships ensure that government trade negotiators focus primarily on the gains that trade rules will bring the corporations, and not on whether the rules are in the wider public interest.

For example in agriculture, companies were involved in designing the WTO trade rules from the very beginning of the negotiating process. Some commentators claim that one US firm which controls half of global trade in grains, actually wrote the first draft of the US government's negotiating position on agriculture before the last round of trade talks.

Corporations were also involved in the negotiation of the WTO TRIPS agreement (see next page for details). This agreement was put on the negotiating agenda by a committee of 13 major corporations which lobbied governments to include their proposals. In the trade talks that followed, 96 out of the 111 members of the US government delegation negotiating the agreement were from corporations. Speaking about business involvement, one Monsanto employee said that 'Industry has identified a major problem in international trade. It crafted a solution, reduced it to a concrete proposal and sold it to our own and other governments.'

Global trade rules are not protecting the earth

- If UK consumption levels were matched globally, we would need eight planets to provide the resources needed.

International trade has contributed to the excessive use of natural resources, as it allows richer countries to consume other nations' resources. For example a huge area – 56 million hectares – of forest was lost globally between 1990 and 1995. And at the rate we are using resources such as petrochemicals and metals, the resulting climate change, health impacts of pollution and habitat damage are already exceeding sustainable levels – and growing as consumption rates increase.

Global trade rules are not democratic

On paper, world trade rules are agreed by 'consensus', meaning that all the 139 WTO members must agree every new rule. In theory this should be ultra-democratic. In practice, however, the important decisions are taken by the European Union, the USA, Japan and Canada. It is their 'consensus' that counts; less powerful nations can take it or leave it!

To make matters worse many developing countries have found themselves overwhelmed by the expense and bureaucracy of endless WTO negotiations. Over half of the poorest countries in the WTO have no representation in Geneva where the WTO HQ is located. These countries have a total population of 81 million people who have effectively no voice at the WTO. Those developing countries that are represented in Geneva often have only one person responsible for all the WTO negotiation, where there can be more than 40 meetings a week. The US has 250 negotiators in Geneva; Bangladesh has one.

Global trade rules are not 'free trade'

'Britain has been a whole-hearted supporter of free trade . . . We remain an unashamed champion of free trade today.'

Tony Blair, World Trade Organisation speech, 1998

Supporters of the WTO, such as the Prime Minister, promote existing trade rules as 'free trade', that is trade that is not restricted by government taxes (called tariffs), limits (called quotas) or bans on particular goods. They claim that free trade benefits both the world economy and poor countries. For example the Department of Trade and Industry says that 'free trade' 'is a key contributor to economic prosperity . . . growth, the creation of new jobs throughout the world, poverty elimination and technological advance'.

Over the last 50 years, trade has indeed become more free as many governments have opened up their economies to foreign trade and investment. At the end of World War II the average tariff (import or export tax) imposed on goods crossing national borders was 40%; now the average is around 4%. However, free trade is not necessarily fair trade. At the end of the last round of trade talks in 1994, it was predicted that Africa would lose $300 – $600 million per year from the agreement. Astonishingly, despite making confident claims for the

benefits of current trade rules, trade officials admit that no one has any clear answer to the simple question: 'have poor countries benefited from the last round of trade negotiations or not?' The research has simply not been done.

More importantly, despite the 'free trade' rhetoric, in reality rich countries only tend to support free trade when they are likely to gain. So while the WTO demands that poor countries remove every possible 'trade barrier', Northern countries keep high import taxes on agriculture and textiles (clothing etc.), areas in which poor countries are most competitive. Overall, Northern countries retain trade barriers that cost developing countries US$700 billion a year in lost income. This is some fourteen times the amount that poor countries receive in aid. Recently the most powerful trading nations failed to agree to 'free trade' access (i.e. no tariffs and quotas) for all exports from the world's 48 poorest countries

The evolution of the the TRIPS (Agreement on Trade Related Intellectual Property rights) rules also graphically illustrates this hypocrisy and how trade rules are being fixed in the interests of big business. The WTO TRIPS agreement has strengthened corporations' rights to control knowledge in ways that are actually contrary to the free trade principles that the WTO rules are supposed to uphold. As such, the TRIPS trade rules have little to do with free trade and plenty to do with corporate profiteering!

People power strikes back! The Battle of Seattle

The rules that govern the current global trading system are deeply unfair. But that hasn't stopped rich countries, spurred on by their multinational corporations, from trying to expand those rules substantially. In November 1999, Ministers from WTO countries met together in Seattle to launch a 'new round' of trade negotiations, to be impressively named the 'Millennium Round'. This new round was to be 'comprehensive', in other words to extend WTO power into many new areas, such as foreign investment. This would have had far-reaching effects for the world's most vulnerable people and for the planet. But, despite having the force of the world's most powerful countries and companies behind it, this attempt did not succeed.

The talks in Seattle collapsed, amidst crippling internal dis-agreement and headline-grabbing external protest. Inside the meeting, developing country governments had had enough of being excluded from the real decision-making process. Outside, pictures of thousands of peaceful protesters being tear-gassed by Robocop-style police were beamed all over the world. Suddenly the WTO was big news. The people on the streets of Seattle were a diverse movement of environmentalists, Southern activists, trade unionists, students, consumers… in fact their diversity reflected the numerous negative impacts of WTO rules, suffered by people across the globe.

This movement took the world, and its leaders, by surprise. The collapse of the talks was heralded as an unprecedented victory for people power. But although Seattle was a real setback for the global rule-makers, they are continuing to push determinedly for WTO expansion.

A dangerous leap into the dark

Western governments, particularly the European Union, are desperate to launch the Millennium Round as soon as possible. The only lessons they seem to have learned from Seattle is that they need to 'sell' the round a bit more effectively to their electorates. In the weary words of Mike Moore, Director-General of the WTO, 'We need to reassure people that globalisation is generally a force for good.' They claim to be moving ever closer to launching a round – critics of the WTO must stay on their toes.

In the meantime, new WTO negotiations have already started on two existing agreements: the Agreement on Agriculture and the General Agreement on Trade in Services (GATS). The GATS negotiations are particularly worrying as the proposed agreement is far-reaching and could result in the privatisation and commercialisation of a whole range of public services, including health and education. The WTO is desperate to rebuild its legitimacy and it is using the GATS to do it.

After Seattle, the UK Secretary of State for Trade and Industry very sensibly recognised that 'the WTO will not be able to continue in its present form. There has to be fundamental and radical change in order for it to meet the needs and aspirations of all of its members.' Such changes have not occurred, yet the world's most powerful people are pushing ahead with WTO expansion anyway, regardless of how this will affect poor people in both North and South, and the global environment. It is deeply irresponsible for governments to behave in this way, and they must not be allowed to do so. There should be no further expansion of WTO rules unless governments can show that such a path would be broadly beneficial to people and the planet. To this end, governments should not proceed until a comprehensive independent assessment of the social and environmental impacts of the last round of trade negotiations has been completed. To do otherwise would be reckless.

Seattle was just the start. The movement that came together to stop the Millennium Round in Seattle continues to grow. This is a historic opportunity for people all over the world to come together and bring about real change on a global level. The People & Planet Trade Justice campaign aims to be part of that change.

Sources: The facts and figures in this document were mainly drawn from research reports by Oxfam, Christian Aid, CAFOD, Friends of the Earth and the Corporate European Observatory.

■ The above information is from People & Planet's website: www.peopleandplanet.org

© *People & Planet*

The stark reality of globalisation

There is first the theory of globalisation. And then there is the reality of it

If all the states 'liberalised' their economies by opening them up to foreign trade and investment, they would all end up benefiting. For in the liberalised global marketplace, each country would focus on those economic activities in which it has a competitive advantage. There would be free movement of resources, personnel, capital and even ideas, and this would lead to prosperity all round.

So the benefits of free trade and the efficiency of free markets are at the core of the globalisation concept. By everyone opening up their borders to the goods and services of all other countries (i.e., abandoning protectionist policies), everybody wins.

That's the theory of it. The reality, unfortunately, is somewhat different. It is perhaps best encapsulated in a passage from the classic *History of the Peloponnesian Wars*, which Greek historian Thucydides wrote around 400BC.

The benefits of free trade and the efficiency of free markets are at the core of the globalisation concepts

---

In it an Athenian envoy addresses a rival delegation as follows: 'You know as well as we do that right, as the world goes, is only a question between equals in power, while the strong do what they can, and the weak suffer what they must.'

As it was with the warring Greek states of those times, so it is with present-day globalisation. Among the great economic powers – principally the US, Japan and the European Union – a degree of fairness can be expected.

Each party is strong enough to retaliate against the others with trade sanctions and prohibitive tariffs if the need arises. For these countries, globalisation is a good thing.

But when it comes to the poor countries of this world, the effects of globalisation have been quite different. Their experience is not one of fair trade, diminished tariffs and free movement of goods and services.

Rather, globalisation means the rich countries with strong economies do as they wish, and the poor countries suffer what they must.

The *New York Times*, to its great credit, has been running a series of editorials over the past few months on how protectionist economic policies in the industrialised nations have a devastating effect on agriculture-based economies of developing countries.

Such policies are mostly due to efforts by agricultural interest groups in the rich countries to ensure their farmers continue to receive generous government subsidies.

Consider cotton. In the *Nation* of June 11, Agriculture Minister Kipruto arap Kirwa was reported to argue that Kenya should revamp the industry to fully exploit the African Growth and Opportunities Act (Agoa).

Urging solutions to the problems posed by crop pests, he declared: 'Cotton is the key to the success of Agoa.' He asked the scientists he was addressing to 'come up with the proper guidelines and recommendations which could boost the development of cotton on the continent'.

Well, the bad news for the minister is that if he ever realises his hopes of reviving cotton growing in Kenya, he will find that this does not bring about the prosperity he anticipates.

In an August 5 editorial with the headline 'The Long Reach of King Cotton', The *New York Times* noted that 'in Burkina Faso, as in neighbouring Mali and Benin, cotton has long been the sole bright spot in the country's ever-dismal economic prospects'.

'White gold, they still call it, though now there is a hint of sarcasm to the expression. Subsidised American cotton farmers now dump so much product on the market that it has driven down world prices.

'So much so that it currently costs Burkina Faso's cotton industry,

traditionally one of the lowest-cost producers, more than the prevailing global price to get a kilo of cotton to the international markets.'

So, while Mr Kirwa is worrying about the effects of pests on cotton, the real problem is that the international cotton prices have been artificially depressed. Even if those scientists were to rid us of the destructive pests, Kenya's cotton (along with Mali's, Benin's and Burkina Faso's) would be priced out of world markets.

Globalisation means the rich countries with strong economies do as they wish, and the poor countries suffer what they must

---

Adding insult onto injury are the comparative numbers of people affected by this policy. Whereas there are only 25,000 American cotton farmers, profiting from those generous subsidies (their average net worth is almost $1 million), the result of this policy of providing subsidies in just one country is 'depressed global prices and a harvest of poverty for Burkina Faso's two million cotton farmers'.

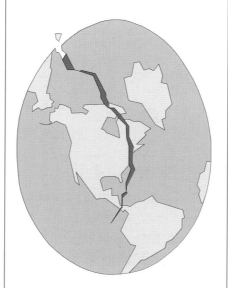

In the editorial titled 'The Rigged Trade Game' (July 20), an example was given which makes the ruling National Rainbow Coalition (Narc)'s promise of 500,000 jobs a year seem more dangerous an illusion than ever.

Apparently the same idea had occurred to leaders of the Philippines back in 1995: 'The (Philippine) government predicted that access to world markets would create a net gain of a half-million farming jobs a year to improve the country's trade balance.'

But it didn't happen: 'No matter how small a wage Filipino workers are willing to accept, they cannot compete with agribusinesses afloat on billions of dollars in government welfare – Instead of making gains, the Philippines lost hundreds of thousands of farming jobs since joining the World Trade Organisation.'

And what is it, according to this distinguished newspaper, that led to this catastrophe for the Philippines? The editorial mentions that 'The US, Europe and Japan funnel nearly a billion dollars a day to their farmers in taxpayer subsidies.'

For those of us who live in the developing countries being pushed around in this way by the big boys, it is comforting to see a paper as influential as *The New York Times* come out to state: 'The glaring credibility gap dividing the developed world's free-trade talk from its market-distorting actions on agriculture cannot be allowed to continue.'

But this does not go far enough. The last word on globalisation must be taken from Shakespeare. In his play *Measure for Measure*, a character makes a point which should be noted by all the industrialised states which are, as *The New York Times* puts it, 'kicking aside the development ladder from some of the world's most desperate people'.

Shakespeare wrote: 'It is excellent to have a giant's strength; but it is tyrannous to use it like a giant.'

From the perspective of poor nations, globalisation as it currently exists is nothing less than a policy of economic tyranny.

© *The National Kenyan Newspaper*

The world for sale

An introduction to corporate globalisation

Corporate globalisation is the spread of big business across the world. As big business gets bigger, it gets more powerful meaning people and governments have less control over their lives. All over the world big business is putting profit before people and the environment.

This is a beginner's guide to corporate globalisation. It looks at some of the impacts of corporate globalisation, the reasons why it's happening, introduces some of the alternatives and suggests what you can do.

What is corporate globalisation?

Corporate globalisation is one kind of globalisation – see box 1. It includes these trends and examples:

- Big companies get bigger and small companies and family businesses struggle to stay open. For example US giant Wal Mart has taken over Asda and Starbucks is taking the place of small coffee shops on every high street;
- Wealth is concentrated in the hands of a few. The gap between poor and rich is growing both between and within countries. Of the 6 billion people in the world, 2.8 billion are living on less than $1.20 a day. More than 60 countries now have lower per capita income than they did in 1990. The 475 richest dollar billionaires have a combined wealth greater than the poorest half of humanity;
- Financial centres such as the City of London have huge amounts of money flowing through them and have control over where money such as our pension funds is invested;
- Governments are forced or persuaded to do what big business wants – money is power and big business uses its power to change laws so that it can carry on growing, even if this means damaging the environment or undermining human rights;

Friends of the Earth

- Multinational companies have been given the right to operate wherever they choose. These rights are enforced by World Trade Organisation (WTO) (see box 3), which has the power to tell governments which laws they can make.

What is new about corporate globalisation?

Today multinationals are more powerful than ever before. In just a few years the number of multinational companies has grown from 37,000 to 60,000 and their affiliates from 170,000 to 800,000. Amongst the 100 largest economic entities, 29 are multinational companies. In other words these companies have bigger economies than most governments.

Foreign investment has grown from $200m in 1990 to $884m in 1999. The UK is now the world's biggest foreign investor which means it has huge power over communities and workers around the world.

Today corporations can set up shop wherever costs are lowest, which usually means wherever labour and environmental standards are lowest. So our clothes are all too often made in sweatshops in the developing world where people are paid a pittance and work under horrific conditions; and ships (such as the *Erika* and *Prestige* which spilt oil off the coasts of France and Spain) are registered in countries with low standards and low taxation, meaning their owners can get away with using old, unsafe ships.

As long as there's money to be made, multinational companies have no qualms about operating in countries with oppressive regimes and governments where human rights abuses abound.

How has corporate globalisation come about?

Governments have allowed corporate globalisation to happen largely because of the successful lobbying of multinational companies. Together governments and companies have devised a one-

size-fits- all prescription for global and national economics. It is based on privatisation – where previously public services are sold to private companies – liberalisation – where free trade (see box 3) is the name of the game – and deregulation – where regulations and standards on health and safety or environmental rules are removed to make it easier to trade. It is about survival of the biggest.

This whole process is controlled, monitored and enforced by organisations like the International Monetary Fund (IMF), World Bank and especially the World Trade Organisation (WTO) (see box 3). These organisations have huge control over what individual countries and communities can and can't do. For example, in order to get World Bank and IMF loans and aid, Mozambique, Tanzania, Cameroon, and Kenya were forced to privatise their water services. European companies like RWE, Suez and Vivendi now 'own' water and water services in parts of these countries and many people cannot afford to pay the prices these companies charge for water.

Unsurprisingly, multinational companies are the main drivers of corporate globalisation. They do this largely through setting up lobby groups. On the international scale, corporate lobby groups have pushed to get global free trade. For example, the World Economic Forum claims it stimulated creation of the WTO, and the European Round-table of Industrialists has been called one of the main driving forces behind the European Single Market.

Friends of the Earth is campaigning against corporate globalisation and for sustainability. Sustainable societies would put people and communities in charge of their fate

In the UK corporate lobbyists have influence over our laws and policies. For example, Lord Richard Holme of the International Chamber of Commerce also sits in the House of Lords where he is able to influence every law passed in Britain. The Confederation of British Industry (CBI) proudly boasts that it 'pushed the government into announcing [planning] reforms that are badly needed and are widely seen as pro-business'. The reforms have tried to remove the public's right to object to damaging development proposals.

Have corporations behaved responsibly?

In a word: no! Many multinational companies claim to be socially and environmentally responsible. They have adopted CSR – Corporate Social Responsibility – which says that companies will be responsible voluntarily. Some companies' practices have improved and some companies are looking to improve even more. But we still hear hundreds of examples of companies abusing

their power in order to make money at the cost of the environment, human rights and communities.

Allowing companies to decide themselves whether or not to behave in a responsible way simply is not working. The market is set up to favour companies that can operate at the lowest cost, and therefore the lowest standards. We need to take positive action to force companies to behave responsibly.

What are the alternatives?

Friends of the Earth is campaigning against corporate globalisation and for sustainability. Sustainable societies would put people and communities in charge of their fate. Our corporate globalisation work looks at three linked areas:

Trade justice

Instead of the current WTO rules that benefit the few at the cost of the many, Friends of the Earth is campaigning for a trade system that:
■ benefits and empowers people,

local communities and supports their livelihoods and protects the resources that they rely on;

- promotes fair (not free) trade between countries, with that trade being conducted in a more sustainable manner and benefits being shared equitably;

- narrows and ultimately eliminates the economic gap between rich and poor in terms of ensuring that the basic needs for life of all people are met.

Corporate accountability

Friends of the Earth is calling for national and international rules and laws to make companies answerable for their actions and to put power back in the hands of citizens and communities. We want citizens and communities to be able to hold multinational companies legally accountable for their bad practices.

In the UK we are campaigning for national rules to hold corporations to account. Along with a coalition of groups, we have introduced a parliamentary bill pressing for real change on corporate accountability. This has received the support of hundreds of MPs, but the Government does not support the contents of the bill.

If companies were properly accountable for their actions, it would help to ensure that people's rights and needs and protection of the environment are given priority over the profits of big business. It

would help to reverse the trend of political power moving away from people and into the hands of multinational companies. It would help ensure that companies operate in the public interest, not against it. It would help protect the environment against rapid destruction for short-term profit. It would help uphold people's rights, livelihoods and ways of life. In short, it would revolutionise the way we do business.

Local economies

The long-term alternative to the one-size-fits-all approach of corporate

Box 3: The WTO and free trade

The WTO is the body that makes and enforces the laws and rules that control international trade (ie trade between different countries). The aim of the WTO is to make trade run as 'freely' as possible so that companies can buy and sell products and services without any barriers in their way. Barriers to trade can include things like environmental standards and health and safety rules, as these can get in the way of making cheap products and low-cost services. For example, if UK citizens demand tough standards on toxic pollution, this would be considered a barrier to foreign companies who may not be able to meet these standards as quickly as domestic companies.

The WTO can overrule national laws that might make trade run less freely. These might be laws designed to protect the environment or human health or tax benefits to support local businesses. The WTO can use fines and sanctions to force countries to get rid of these protective measures. As a result, governments hold back from policies that might conflict with WTO rules. For example, the UK Government does not buy only sustainably sourced timber because this may breach trade rules.

The US and EU dominate the WTO. They arrive at meetings with hundreds of delegates. Developing countries cannot even afford to follow every aspect of the negotiations

globalisation will also be about supporting the development and rejuvenation of local economies.

What you can do

Join our email activists' list to take simple actions against the destructive activities of multinational companies and to help us challenge corporate power. To join, visit www.bigbusinessexposed.com

- The above information is from Friends of the Earth. For further information visit their website at www.foe.co.uk Alternatively, see page 41 for their address details.

© Friends of the Earth

Fairtrade retail sales

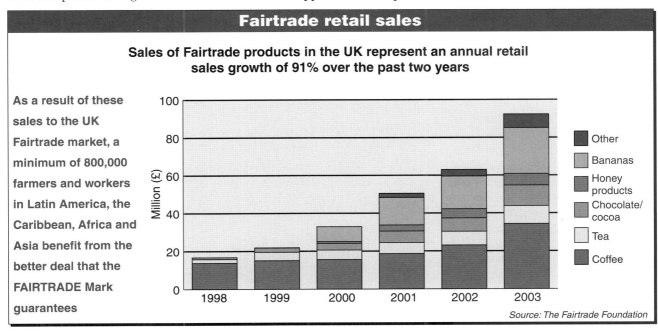

Sales of Fairtrade products in the UK represent an annual retail sales growth of 91% over the past two years

As a result of these sales to the UK Fairtrade market, a minimum of 800,000 farmers and workers in Latin America, the Caribbean, Africa and Asia benefit from the better deal that the FAIRTRADE Mark guarantees

Legend: Other, Bananas, Honey products, Chocolate/cocoa, Tea, Coffee

Million (£): 0, 20, 40, 60, 80, 100

Years: 1998, 1999, 2000, 2001, 2002, 2003

Source: The Fairtrade Foundation

Power hungry

Six reasons to regulate global food corporations

Global food companies have grown too powerful and are undermining the fight against poverty in developing countries. They are draining wealth from rural communities, marginalising small-scale farming, and infringing people's rights. Urgent action is needed to re-govern agricultural markets so they benefit poor people, and to make companies legally accountable for their impacts on human rights and the environment.

Transnational corporations (TNCs) such as Monsanto, Cargill, Nestlé and Wal-Mart have come to dominate supply chains for food and agricultural goods, from seed to supermarket shelf. Two decades of economic liberalisation have enabled 'agrifood' TNCs to expand enormously in size, power and influence in developing countries; as a result, they now deal more directly with small-scale farmers. A wave of mergers, acquisitions and business alliances in the agrifood industry has concentrated enormous market power amongst these corporations:

- the top 30 food retailing corporations account for one-third of global grocery sales
- one TNC controls 80% of Peru's milk production
- five companies control 90% of the world grain trade
- six corporations control three-quarters of the global pesticides market.

Agrifood TNCs are rapidly transforming agricultural systems in developing countries, which play a vital role in reducing poverty and promoting food security. Seventy per cent of the world's poor people live and work in rural areas, and the majority will continue to do so until well into the 21st century. But instead of helping to generate vibrant farm economies, TNCs are having anti-development impacts on rural communities, and are undermining poor people's basic rights.

act:onaid
international

This report marks the beginning of ActionAid International's engagement with governments and civil society on agrifood industry regulation. It highlights six reasons to regulate agrifood TNCs:

1 TNCs use and abuse their market power to drain wealth from poor communities

Agrifood TNCs are exercising their market power to raise the price of agricultural inputs, engage in unfair buying practices, form price-fixing cartels, shut local companies out of markets, and push down prices for farmers' goods. The UK supermarket Asda Wal-Mart, for example, used its bargaining power over suppliers to cut the price of bananas in 2002. Other retailers followed suit and demanded deep price reductions from their suppliers. By 2004 bananas were retailing at £0.74 per kg in the UK, down from £1.08 in 2002. This meant that growers in Costa Rica would not have been able to get the legal minimum price for a box of bananas, or pay plantation workers the legal minimum wage. Eighty-five per cent of all recent fines imposed on global price-fixing cartels were paid by agrifood companies. Corporations such as Tate & Lyle, Cargill and Archer Daniels Midland have between them paid out over one billion dollars to settle price-fixing lawsuits brought against them.

2 TNCs pay low prices and capture the resulting value

Many factors can work to bring down farm prices in addition to the misuse of market power, including oversupply and changes in trade rules. Despite dramatic falls in the prices for important farm goods bought by TNCs such as coffee, rice, sugar, milk, wheat and tea, consumers often do not pay less for these products. Whether they actively force down farmgate prices, or take advantage of depressed markets to pay low prices, agrifood TNCs often keep the profits for themselves. The gap between farm and retail prices is growing, and is wider in countries where TNCs have concentrated market power. The World Bank estimates that the farm-retail price gap is costing commodity-exporting countries more than US$100 billion each year, and that anti-competitive behaviour by agrifood TNCs is a key cause.

3 TNCs marginalise poor farmers and rural workers

The agrifood corporations' market power allows them to set the 'rules of the game': who's in and who's out of the supply chain. By imposing tough standards that poor farmers cannot afford to meet, TNCs are threatening the livelihoods of hundreds of thousands of smallholders. After a series of aggressive takeovers in Brazil, for example, Nestlé and Parmalat forced over 50,000 dairy farmers out of their supply chains; as a result, many went out of business altogether. Women make up to 90% of the labour force in the supply chains for fruit and vegetables exported from developing countries. Agrifood TNCs are forcing the costs and risks of doing business onto suppliers, who in turn pass on these pressures by undermining women workers' rights.

4 TNCs are not fully accountable for their impacts on human rights and the environment

Agrifood TNCs frequently violate poor people's basic rights. In India, for example, at least 12,000 children worked on farms in 2003 supplying cotton seeds to subsidiaries of TNCs including Bayer, Monsanto, Syngenta and Unilever. But TNCs have in many respects outgrown the reach of national law in many of the countries in which they do business. Domestic laws are patchy and unevenly applied in poor countries, and TNCs can avoid prosecution by exploiting the legal separation between parent companies and their subsidiaries. TNCs are operating in what amounts to a 'regulatory void' in which they can weaken labour, environmental and public health laws, and practise double standards by behaving more responsibly in countries with tighter regulation, and less responsibly elsewhere.

5 Corporate social responsibility is optional and insufficient

Voluntary efforts by companies to improve their social and environmental performance – a practice known as 'corporate social responsibility' (CSR) – have important benefits, such as helping companies to develop and implement best practice within their industry sector. But companies' goodwill alone has proved insufficient to the task of protecting human rights and the environment. The sheer number of company and industry-wide codes is hindering companies' efforts to tackle the issues, and is creating uncertainty as to which standard they should use. Most CSR initiatives have been undertaken by large firms with high public profiles. The agricultural

sector has relatively few company codes, and the food manufacturing industry even less. The selection – or indeed avoidance – of issues covered by a CSR code varies significantly, and many companies have adopted a 'pick-and-mix' approach. Most codes are general statements of principles rather than detailed instructions as to how these principles might be applied. Meanwhile, out of an estimated 64,000 TNCs operating today, only 1,500-2,000 – 3% at most – produce annual CSR reports.

6 People harmed by corporate activity are denied access to justice

When TNCs violate human rights and the environment, affected communities look for redress through the laws of their own country, or in the country where the company is headquartered. There are also a number of international treaties that affected people could use. Yet national authorities are often unwilling or unable to prosecute companies, while there are no international mechanisms for redress that are legally binding on companies. People harmed by corporate activity are often poor, and yet in most cases they must bear the costs of bringing litigation against corporations. Claimants may fear persecution, particularly if the company has been collaborating with the government or security forces. If affected people do manage to bring a legal case, however, they can wait years for redress because companies

---

Transnational corporations (TNCs) have come to dominate supply chains for food and agricultural goods, from seed to supermarket shelf

---

have greater legal, political and financial resources to delay and weaken any decision.

Solutions

Many rural communities are mobilising to defend their interests against the negative impacts of agrifood TNCs through grassroots action. ActionAid actively supports such initiatives, including co-operatives and producer organisations. Governments and international institutions should also take action to ensure TNCs do not infringe the rights of poor and excluded communities. Countervailing measures should be seen not simply as a response to the misuse of corporate power. They are also important tools for building a more democratic and equitable food system, and for generating sustainable growth with equity. ActionAid International calls on governments to:

1) Re-govern agrifood markets towards pro-poor development goals by:
- preventing the misuse of TNC buyer power in agrifood markets
- strengthening, and where appropriate establishing, rural producer organisations
- addressing the global agricultural commodity crisis affecting small-scale farming communities.

2) Hold TNCs legally accountable for their impacts on human rights and the environment by:
- ensuring that TNCs fulfil their obligations to promote, secure and protect human rights under the UN Human Rights Norms for Business
- introducing and enforcing domestic legislation to regulate TNC activities in developing countries
- building capacity in developing countries among farmer organisations and civil society groups.

■ The above information is from the executive summary of *Power hungry – six reasons to regulate global food corporations*, a report from ActionAid. For more information see their website which can be found at www.actionaid.org.uk

© ActionAid International

Free trade leaves world food in grip of global giants

Global food companies are aggravating poverty in developing countries by dominating markets, buying up seed firms and forcing down prices for staple goods including tea, coffee, milk, bananas and wheat, according to a report launched 27 January 2005.

As 50,000 people marched through Porto Alegre, in southern Brazil, to mark the opening of the annual World Social Forum on developing country issues, the report from ActionAid was set to highlight how power in the world food industry has become concentrated in a few hands.

The report will say that 30 companies now account for a third of the world's processed food; five companies control 75% of the international grain trade; and six companies manage 75% of the global pesticide market.

It finds that two companies dominate sales of half the world's bananas, three trade 85% of the world's tea, and one, Wal-mart, now controls 40% of Mexico's retail food sector. It also found that Monsanto controls 91% of the global GM seed market.

Household names including Nestlé, Monsanto, Unilever, Tesco, Wal-mart, Bayer and Cargill are all said to have expanded hugely in size, power and influence in the past decade directly because of the trade liberalisation policies being advanced by the US, Britain and other G8 countries whose leaders met in Davos in January.

'A wave of mergers and business alliances has concentrated market power in very few hands,' the report says.

It accuses the companies of shutting local companies out of the market, driving down prices, setting international and domestic trade rules to suit themselves, imposing tough standards that poor farmers cannot meet, and charging consumers more.

By John Vidal in Porto Alegre

The report says 85% of all the recent fines imposed on global cartels were paid by agrifood companies, with three of them forced to pay out $500m (£266m) to settle price-fixing lawsuits.

'It is a dangerous situation when so few companies control so many lives,' said John Samuel of ActionAid.

> ### 30 companies now account for a third of the world's processed food; five companies control 75% of the international grain trade

The ActionAid report argues that many food behemoths are wealthier than the countries in which they do their business. Nestlé, it says, recorded profits greater than Ghana's GDP in 2002, Unilever profits were a third larger than the national income of Mozambique and Walmart profits are bigger than the economies of both countries combined.

The companies are also said to be taking advantage of the collapse in farm prices. Prices for coffee, cocoa, rice, palm oil and sugar have fallen by more than 50% in the past 20 years.

The report feeds into growing calls at Porto Alegre for the regulation of multinational food companies. A coalition of the largest international environmental, trade and human rights groups, including Greenpeace, Friends of the Earth, Amnesty, Via Campesina and Focus on the Global South, said they would be working together to press for corporate accountability.

Retailers such as Tesco, Ahold, Carrefour and Metro are buying increasing volumes of fruit, vegetables, meat and dairy products in developing countries, but their exacting food safety and environmental standards are driving small farmers out of business, says ActionAid.

A spokeswoman for the Food and Drink Federation, which represents British food businesses, recognised that the industry's success 'is closely linked to those at the beginning of the food supply chain'.

But she added: 'Britain, the world's fourth largest food importing country, invests heavily and provides an enormous market for developing world farmers.'

Trade justice campaign

The basics

Why campaign on trade?

Half the world's population are living in poverty and the gap between rich and poor is widening. But it doesn't have to be this way. We can change it – by making international trade work for the poor so they have a chance to work their way out of poverty. That's what the Trade Justice Campaign is all about.

The slavery of free trade

Kofi is a victim of free trade. He earns £1 a day breaking rocks to make gravel. He used to be a tomato farmer. But that livelihood, which bought food for his family and schooling for his children, has been taken away from him.

Free trade means a country's economy is run without government intervention. It is a policy that rich country governments and international institutions are forcing poor countries to accept.

Free trade is imposed on poor countries through:

- agreements between two or more countries
- conditions and 'economic advice' given to poor countries in return for loans from the International Monetary Fund (IMF) and the World Bank
- agreements at the World Trade Organisation.

The effects of free trade can be seen across the developing world. Millions of poor people's livelihoods are being threatened, and their governments are powerless to prevent it.

If we are serious about having a world free from poverty, then poor countries must be given the chance to work their own way out of poverty.

Trade could be that chance.

What we're calling for

We need to persuade the UK government that, to end poverty and protect the environment, we need trade justice – not free trade.

Christian Aid
We believe in life before death

We need to change the rules that govern international trade so that poor countries have the freedom to help and support their vulnerable farmers and industries.

To do this we need to campaign to persuade the UK government to support trade justice not free trade. And they need to use their influence to call for change within the international institutions that govern trade policy.

Christian Aid is also a member of the Trade Justice Movement – a broad and powerful coalition of charities and campaigning organisations who all believe it's time to change the way the world trades.

Five immediate demands of the campaign

1. Stop the EU's free-trade agreements with former colonies

The EU is currently negotiating a trade agreement with 77 former colonies. As part of this agreement, poor countries will have to accept an Economic Partnership Agreement that opens their markets further and limits the help they can give farmers and industry.

2. An end to the IMF and World Bank setting poor countries' trade policies

The IMF and World Bank have enormous power over poor countries.

They use conditions attached to loans to promote free trade.

The UK treasury and department for international development should use their influence at these institutions to argue for an end to these conditions.

3. Special treatment for poor countries at the WTO

WTO agreements should be biased in favour of poor countries, so that they have a better chance of using trade as a way out of poverty. This has already been agreed in principle at the WTO, but needs to be enforced.

4. Cut the massive export subsidies used in rich countries

Subsidies for exporters must be ended because of their devastating impact on developing country markets.

Subsidies of rich countries must be reformed to meet the social and environmental needs of both rich and poor countries.

5. Debt cancellation and aid increases must not be used to further impose free trade

Poor countries still need aid and further debt cancellation to help strengthen their economies. But this will be undermined if they are forced to accept free trade conditions, increasing their dependence on the rich world.

Who we're calling on

Our main target is the UK government. We want them to use their influence within the powerful international institutions (that's the EU, the World Trade Organisation and World Bank/International Monetary Fund) to call for change.

We campaign directly to the UK government (particularly Prime Minister Tony Blair, Trade and Industry Secretary Patricia Hewitt, and International Development Secretary Hilary Benn) and through MPs.

We lobby as an organisation and we also encourage people like you to use your voices for change by taking action – like sending postcards, writing letters or attending events.

Top 10 facts

1. International trade is worth $10 million a minute.

2. But poor countries only account for 0.4 per cent of this trade. Since 1980 their share has halved.

3. Rigged trade rules cost the developing world $700 billion a year, according to the UN.

4. Income per person in the poorest countries in Africa has fallen by a quarter in the last 20 years.

5. The three richest people in the world control more wealth than all 600 million people living in the world's poorest countries.

6. Nearly half the world's population (2.8 billion people) live on less than US$2 per day.

7. The prices of many poor countries' key exports are at a 150-year low.

8. The world's 50 poorest countries have less than three per cent of the vote at the International Monetary Fund, an institution whose financial decisions spell life and death for ordinary people around the globe. Just one country – the US – has sole veto power.

9. At one full meeting of the WTO, the EU had 500 negotiators. Haiti had none.

10. After one round of trade negotiations, rich countries calculated that they would be $141.8 billion better off, while Africa would lose $2.6 billion.

■ The above information is from Christian Aid's website which can be found at www.christian-aid.org.uk

© Christian Aid. Used with permission

Half of all workers on $2 a day or less

By Charlotte Moore

A record number of people are working in the global economy but half of them make $2 a day or less, according to a report published 7 December 2004.

The International Labour Organisation's *World Employment* report said about 2.8 billion people were employed globally in 2003. But nearly 1.4 billion, the highest number ever, are living on less than $2 a day, while 550 million are living under the $1 poverty line. On current growth projections, this could halve in some areas of the world by 2015.

China, south-east Asia and south Asia are most likely to reach the goal of halving the proportion of people living on $1 a day but this is unlikely to be achieved in Latin America and the Caribbean. Sub-Saharan Africa is significantly off-track. Only east Asia has a realistic chance of halving the numbers living on $2 a day.

The ILO said the world needs to focus on economic policies that create decent and productive employment opportunities if the Millennium Development Goals are to be achieved.

One of the main goals is to halve the number people living on $1 a day by 2015. About 185.9 million people worldwide were unemployed in 2003. This is just the 'tip of iceberg', the report says, since more than seven times that number are employed but still live in poverty.

To achieve high employment rates and a greater reduction in poverty, there needs to be a focus on improving productivity. Gains in productivity can benefit workers in the form of higher earnings and reduced working time.

The reality of globalisation means employees sometimes lose their jobs, says the report. Institutions should provide security and training to better prepare the workforce for the changing labour market.

Director-general Juan Somavia said: 'Women and men all over the world expect to get a fair chance at a decent job.'

© Guardian Newspapers Limited 2004

Analysing inequality

Is globalisation widening the gap between rich and poor? No. The gap has narrowed during the last two decades

It is often claimed that the gap between rich and poor has been widening over recent decades and that the living conditions of the poor have deteriorated as a result of globalisation. A recurrent figure, drawn from the 1999 Human Development Report of the United Nations Development Programme (UNDP), gives an alarming account: 'Gaps in income between the poorest and richest people and countries have continued to widen. In 1960 the 20% of the world's people in the richest countries had 30 times the income of the poorest 20% – in 1997, 74 times as much.'

Correcting the record

New research disproves such claims and sheds a much more favourable light on the contribution of global economic integration to incomes and income distribution. In a study for the National Bureau of Economic Research, Xavier Sala-i-Martin points out that the UNDP report computed its poverty ratios by simply comparing unadjusted incomes, thus ignoring the fact that the cost of living is lower in developing countries.[1] Once adjusted for purchasing power parity, the poverty ratio of the richest 20% to the poorest 20% has actually started to diminish over the last two decades, according to Sala-i-Martin. 'Rather than rising from 20 to 74, the ratio increases from 11.3 in 1960 to 15.9 in 1980, but then declines slowly to 15.09 in 1998.'

Massive poverty reduction

Using nine different indexes to measure income distribution between individuals, Sala-i-Martin shows that there has been a substantial narrowing of the gap between rich and poor during the last two decades. Other studies by Surjit Bhalla[2] and Arne Melchior[3] reach similar conclusions. This decline in global inequalities is mainly the result

International Chamber of Commerce
The world business organization

of massive poverty reduction in countries such as India and China, which account for 38% of the world's population, and other large developing countries. Bhalla estimates that the proportion of people in the world living on less than a dollar a day has fallen from 30% in 1987 to 13.1% in 2000. In Asia, more than 650 million people were lifted out of deep poverty between 1970 and 2000.

Quality of life

When measuring poverty, it is important to take into account living

---

'In 1960 the 20% of the world's people in the richest countries had 30 times the income of the poorest 20% – in 1997, 74 times as much'

---

standards and not just incomes. Here again, the evidence is that, overall, quality of life has improved in the developing world. According to the Australian Department of Foreign Affairs and Trade, the number of undernourished people in the world has been reduced from 920 million in 1970 to 810 million today. A World Bank study says that school enrolments in Uganda doubled during the 1990s. In a report for the Brookings Institution Global Inequality Group, Gary Burtless shows that life expectancy has been rising almost everywhere in the world and that as a result 'world inequality in the distribution of expected life spans has declined'.[4]

Domestic factors

The purpose here is not to give a picture that is rosier than reality. Many countries have suffered from increased marginalisation and have been unable to reduce poverty over the last two decades. More than 40% of Africans live on less than a dollar a day, a proportion that has been steadily increasing in the continent as a whole since the 1970s. Conflict and bad govern-

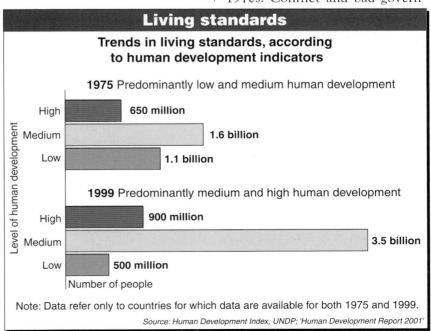

Living standards

Trends in living standards, according to human development indicators

1975 Predominantly low and medium human development

High — 650 million
Medium — 1.6 billion
Low — 1.1 billion

1999 Predominantly medium and high human development

High — 900 million
Medium — 3.5 billion
Low — 500 million

Number of people

Level of human development

Note: Data refer only to countries for which data are available for both 1975 and 1999.

Source: Human Development Index, UNDP; 'Human Development Report 2001'

ance persist in holding many African countries back from economic progress.

The number of undernourished people in the world has been reduced from 920 million in 1970 to 810 million today

---

Inequalities have also increased *within* several countries with high levels of growth. For example, rapid economic growth in China has widened the gap between rural and urban areas. But as a World Bank report points out, 'if this increase of inequality in China has been the price of growth, it has paid off in terms of massive reduction of poverty'. In fact, income distribution in a given country primarily depends on domestic factors such as economic policy choices and redistribution mechanisms.

References

1 Xavier Sala-i-Martin, *The Disturbing 'Rise' of Global Income Inequality*, National Bureau of Economic Research, Working Paper 8904, 2002 and *The World Distribution of Income (estimated from individual country distributions)*, National Bureau of Economic Research, Working Paper 8933, 2002

2 Surjit Bhalla , *Imagine There's No Country: Poverty, Inequality and Growth in the Era of Globalisation*, Institute for International Economics, 2002

3 Arne Melchior, 'Global Income Inequality. Beliefs, facts and unresolved issues', *World Economics*, Vol. 2, No 3, July-September 2001

4 Gary Burtless, *Is the Global Gap between Rich and Poor Getting Wider?*, The Brookings Institution, June 2002

■ The above information is an extract from *Standing up for the global economy*, published by the International Chamber of Commerce. For further information, visit their website at www.iccwbo.org

© *International Chamber of Commerce (ICC)*

How do people in different parts of the world view globalisation?

The majority say it is a good thing

Polls conducted to sound out public opinion on globalisation concur: an overwhelming majority of people almost everywhere think globalisation is good for them and their country. Some of the findings are particularly telling:

■ A survey of 25,000 citizens across 25 countries – 14 of them in the developing world – shows that close to 75% believe globalisation improves their lives and those of their families.[1]

■ According to another worldwide survey, support for globalisation is strongest in Nigeria (90%), South Korea (84%) and Kenya (82%), followed closely by Indonesia (79%), Vietnam (79%) and China (76%). In South Africa and Uganda, four out of 10 even see globalisation as a *very* good thing.[2]

■ In North America and Western Europe, most people also have a positive view of globalisation, but opposition is stronger than in the developing world. In the European Union, 63% say they are in favour of globalisation, 29% against.[3]

■ In France, six out of 10 think globalisation is good for their country, while 36% have a negative opinion – the largest percentage among wealthy countries.

■ Globalisation is more popular among the young. In France, 72% of those below 30 years of age say globalisation is a good thing, compared to 58% of respondents older than 50. More than 60% of young Peruvians view globalisation favourably, compared with only a third of those their parents' age.

■ In a recent survey conducted in the US, two-thirds of respondents agreed with the following statement: 'I favour free trade, and I believe it is necessary for the government to have programs to help workers who lose their jobs'. Only 18% advocated free trade in the absence of such help.[4]

■ In sub-Saharan Africa, 75% of households think it is a good thing that multinational companies are investing in their countries.

■ Nearly six out of 10 Nigerians (58%) and majorities in Vietnam (55%), Pakistan (55%) and Uganda (53%) say that the growth of trade and business has been very good for themselves and their families.

References

1 Environics International/World Economic Forum, *Global Public Opinion on Globalisation*, 2002

2 The Pew Research Center, *Pew Global Attitudes Project: Views of a Changing World*, 2003

3 Eurobarometer/European Commission, *Globalisation*, 2003

4 Program on International Policy Attitudes, *Americans on Globalisation: A Study of U.S. Public Attitudes*, March 2000

■ The above information is an extract from *Standing up for the global economy*, published by the International Chamber of Commerce. For further information, visit their website which can be found at www.iccwbo.org

© *International Chamber of Commerce*

Poverty or prosperity

Is either caused by globalisation?

There are advocates of globalisation, opponents of globalisation, and a wide middle which sees globalisation as nearly inevitable, largely positive, and in need of sensible management. The single issue which seems to most divide these groups is the role globalisation plays in causing or curing global poverty. The advocates say globalisation brings the first real chance of prosperity to the impoverished corners of the world.

Opponents say globalisation is the cause of growing poverty and inequality on the planet. And those in the middle see how unbridled globalisation could wreak havoc on some while simultaneously opening the doors of opportunity to others.

I can't reconcile these vastly different views. But I can give you the broad outlines of the debate so you can see where you fall. And if you already know your role in this argument, maybe this information will help you more clearly see the other side's point of view.

Below are quotes from larger documents dealing with globalisation and poverty. I have chosen short excerpts and arranged them in order from the most pro-globalisation to the most anti-globalisation.

> Globalisation advocates assert that it brings the first real chance of prosperity to the impoverished corners of the world. Opponents say globalisation is the cause of growing poverty and inequality on the planet. And those in the middle see how unbridled globalisation could wreak havoc on some while simultaneously opening the doors of opportunity to others.

'Globalisation, then, is growth-promoting. Growth, in turn, reduces poverty . . . the liberalisation of international transactions is good for freedom and prosperity. The anti-liberal critique is wrong: marginalisation is in large part caused by not enough rather than too much globalisation.'

Razeen Sally,
London School of Economics

'Agreements like NAFTA and the WTO force nations to respect contracts, which encourages responsible investment and, hence, economic growth. And, you see, economic growth creates a middle class, and a middle class, eventually, demands democracy. That is the story of the 20th century and, God willing, it will be the story of the 21st.'

Jonah Goldberg, Editor,
National Review Online

'Personally, I do not believe that those [poor] people are victims of globalisation. Their problem is not that they are included in the global market but, in most cases, that they are excluded from it.'

Kofi Annan

'I believe that the ultimate logic of globalisation will eventually win out; and most, and perhaps even all nations will eventually cross the threshold of democracy and transparent market economies. However, I also believe this will be the work of generations, and that there may be substantial backsliding in the process.'

James C. Bennett

'Globalisation is generating great wealth. This could be used to massively reduce poverty worldwide and to reduce global inequality. The world's richest 225 people have a combined wealth equal to the annual income of the poorest 47 per cent of the world's people. We must try to manage this new era, in a way which reduces these glaring inequalities and that helps to lift millions of people out of poverty.'

Clare Short, Former UK
Secretary of State for
International Development

'Globalisation has helped re-duce poverty in a large number of developing countries but it must be

Labour market and economic indicators

	Unemployment rate %			Employment-to-population ratio %	
	1994	2003	2004	1994	2004
World	5.5	6.3	6.1	62.4	61.8
Developed economies and EU	8.2	7.4	7.2	55.9	56.0
Central and E. Europe (non-EU) and Commonwealth of Independent States	6.5	8.4	8.3	56.5	51.6
East Asia	2.5	3.3	3.3	78.2	76.4
South-East Asia and the Pacific	4.1	6.5	6.4	66.8	66.7
South Asia	4.0	4.8	4.7	56.2	56.1
Latin America and the Caribbean	7.0	9.3	8.6	55.6	56.0
Middle East and North Africa	12.4	11.7	11.7	43.9	47.3
Sub-Saharan Africa	9.8	10.0	10.1	65.5	65.6

Source: ILO Global Employment Trends Model, 2005; IMF, World Economic Outlook 2004

harnessed better to help the world's poorest, most marginalised countries improve the lives of their citizens, according to the report *Globalisation, Growth and Poverty: Building an Inclusive World Economy*.'

The World Bank

'There needs to be a better balance between the role of markets and the role of government. Simplistic reforms based on free-market ideology don't work. The way that East Asia managed globalisation, which combined an export-orientation with policies aimed at poverty reduction, worked even for the poor people.

These countries did liberalise trade, but only as they created jobs.'

Joseph E. Stiglitz,
2001 winner of the Nobel
Prize for Economics

'A permanent worldwide underclass is in danger of emerging, especially in developing countries, making it increasingly difficult to build the political consensus on which domestic stability, international peace and globalisation itself depend.'

Henry Kissinger

'The evidence strongly suggests that global income inequality has risen in the last twenty years. The standards of measuring this change, and the reasons for it, are contested – but the trend is clear. The "champagne glass" effect implies that advocacy of globalisation is not enough: international organisations need to move beyond integration into the world economy as the primary goal of policy.'

Robert Wade,
London School of Economics

'Obscene patterns of poverty and inequalities amidst ostentatious wealth are thus the very stuff of our global system. They raise basic issues of morality and ethics for the prosperous areas of the world. We need to be asking whether the current inequalities are legitimate and just? Can something be done to achieve some degree of human decency?'

Robert Fatton, Jr.
University of Virginia

'Neoliberal economic globalisation encourages the pursuit of profit regardless of social and environmental costs. It is associated with increasing levels of inequality, both between and within countries; the concentration of resources and power in fewer and fewer hands (resulting in an erosion of democracy); economic, social, political and economic exclusion; economic instability; spiralling rates of natural resource exploitation; and a loss of biological and cultural diversity.'

Friends of the Earth

Global governance in crisis

Global economy 'must adjust to include millions it puts in poverty'. UN labour organisation seeks political will for a new ethical thrust

World leaders must address the 'ethical vaccuum' at the heart of globalisation or face the danger that the widening gap between rich and poor will lead to further conflict, political upheaval and war, the International Labour Organisation said 24 February 2004.

Its year-long commission on globalisation has concluded that the deep-seated and persistent imbalances in the workings of the global economy are unsustainable.

Without fairer rules governing trade flows, immigration and labour standards, billions will continue to miss out on the rising global prosperity, prompting a fresh wave of international instability.

'Global governance is in crisis,' the report said. 'We are at a critical juncture and we need urgently to rethink our current policies and institutions. The economy is becoming increasingly global, while social and political institutions remain largely local, national or regional.'

By Charlotte Denny,
Economics Correspondent

Properly managed globalisation could be a force for good: the faster growth spurred by integrating world markets has the potential to lift millions out of poverty.

'The economy is becoming increasingly global, while social and political institutions remain largely local, national or regional'

'Wisely managed, it can deliver unprecedented material progress, generate more productive and better jobs for all, and contribute significantly to reducing world poverty.'

But to achieve this will require world leaders' political will to change the current path of globalisation.

'Wealth is being created, but too many countries and people are not sharing its benefits.'

Some of the poorest states suffer from too little not too much integration with world markets, the ILO's director general, Juan Somavia, said.

'Globalisation has passed over the heads of African countries.'

The panel, which was chaired by the presidents of Tanzania and Finland and included the Nobel prize-winning economist Joseph Stiglitz, interviewed citizens, politicians and business leaders from around the world.

It found widespread concern about the current direction of globalisation. 'Its advantages are too distant for many while its risks are all too real,' the report said.

'Corruption is widespread. Open societies are threatened by global

---

terrorism, and the future of open markets is increasingly in question.'

Globalisation had created winners and losers both within and between countries. Unemployment worldwide had reached 185m, according to the ILO, the highest recorded. And the richest 1% of the US population raked in 17% of the country's income, the highest level of income inequality since the 1920s.

On the positive side, the rapid rise in global communications brought the reality of life in the poorest communities on to the TV screens of the rich, prompting growing concern in the west about fairer trade rules and global labour standards.

'A truly global conscience is beginning to emerge, sensitive to the inequities of poverty, gender discrimination, child labour and environmental degradation wherever they occur.'

The report recommended that western leaders tackle the skewed rules of global trade which shut exports from some of the poorest countries out of rich countries'

markets and promote a minimum level of social protection worldwide.

More aid money had to be found to finance the UN's ambitious millennium development aim to halve global poverty by 2015.

'The choice is clear,' the report said.

'We can correct the global governance deficit in the world today, ensure accountability and adopt coherent policies that forge a path for globalisation that is fair and just, both within and between countries; or we can prevaricate and risk a slide into further spirals of insecurity, political turbulence, conflicts and wars.'

10 ways to democratise the global economy

Information from the Global Exchange

Citizens can and should play an active role in shaping the future of our global economy. Here are some of the ways in which we can work together to reform global trade rules, demand that corporations are accountable to people's needs, build strong and free labour and promote fair and environmentally sustainable alternatives.

1. No globalisation without representation

Multilateral institutions such as the World Trade Organization, the World Bank, and the International Monetary Fund create global policy with input mainly from multinational corporations and very little input from grassroots citizens' groups. We need to ensure that all global citizens must be democratically represented in the formulation, implementation, and evaluation of all global social and economic policies of the WTO, the IMF, and the WB. The WTO must immediately halt all meetings and negotiations in order for a full, fair, and public assessment to be conducted of the impacts of the

WTO's policies to date. The WTO must be replaced by a body that is fully democratic, transparent, and accountable to citizens of the entire world instead of to corporations. We must build support for trade policies that protect workers, human rights, and the environment.

2. Mandate corporate responsibility

Corporations have so heavily influenced global trade negotiations

that they now have rights and representation greater than individual citizens and even governments. Under the guise of 'free trade' they advocate weakening of labour and environmental laws – a global economy of sweatshops and environmental devastation. Corporations must be subject to the people's will; they should have to prove their worth to society or be dismantled. Corporations must be accountable to public needs, be open to public scrutiny, provide living wage jobs, abide by all environmental and labour regulations, and be subject to all laws governing them. Shareholder activism is an excellent tool for challenging corporate behaviour.

3. Restructure the global financial architecture

Currency speculation and the derivatives market move over $1.5 trillion daily (compared to world trade of $6 trillion annually), earning short-term profits for wealthy investors at the expense of long-term development. Many countries are beginning to implement 'capital controls' in order to regulate the influence of foreign capital, and grassroots groups are advocating the restructuring and regulation of the global financial architecture. Citizens can pass local city resolutions for the Tobin Tax – a tax of .1% to .25% on currency transactions which would provide a disincentive for speculation but not affect real capital investment, and create a huge fund for building schools and clinics throughout the world.

4. Cancel all debt, end structural adjustment and defend economic sovereignty

Debt is crushing most poor countries' ability to develop as they spend huge amounts of their resources servicing odious debt rather than serving the needs of their populations. Structural adjustment is the tool promoted by the IMF and World Bank to keep countries on schedule with debt payments, with programmes promoting export-led development at the expense of social needs. There is an international movement demanding that all debt be cancelled in the year 2000 in order for countries to prioritise health care, education, and real development. Countries must have the autonomy to pursue their own economic plans, including prioritising social needs over the needs of multinational corporations.

5. Prioritise human rights – including economic rights – in trade agreements

The United Nations must be the strongest multilateral body – not the WTO. The US must ratify all

international conventions on social and political rights. Trade rules must comply with higher laws on human rights as well as economic and labour rights included in the United Nations Declaration of Human Rights. We should promote alternative trade agreements that include fair trade, debt cancellation, micro-credit, and local control over development policies.

6. Promote sustainable development – not consumption – as the key to progress

Global trade and investment should not be ends in themselves, but rather the instruments for achieving equitable and sustainable development, including protection for workers and the environment. Global trade agreements should not undermine the ability of each nation, state or local community to meet its citizens' social, environmental, cultural or economic needs. International development should not be export-driven, but rather should prioritise food security, sustainability, and democratic participation.

7. Integrate women's needs in all economic restructuring

Women make up half the world but hold less than 5% of positions of power in determining global economic policy, and own an estimated 1% of global property. Family survival around the world depends on the economic independence of women. Economic policies need to take into account women's important role in nutrition, education, and development. This includes access to family planning as well as education, credit, job training, policy decision-making, and other needs.

8. Build free and strong labour unions internationally and domestically

As trade becomes more 'free,' labour unions are still restricted from organising in most countries. The International Labour Organization should have the same enforcement power as the WTO. The US should ratify ILO conventions and set an example in terms of enforcing workers' rights to organise and bargain collectively. As corporations increase their multinational strength, unions are working to build bridges across borders and organise globally. Activists can support their efforts and ensure that free labour is an essential component of any 'free trade' agreements.

9. Develop community control over capital; promote socially responsible investment

Local communities should not be beholden to the IMF, international capital, multinational corporations, or any other non-local body for policy. Communities should be able to develop investment and development programmes that suit local needs including passing anti-sweatshop purchasing restrictions, promoting local credit unions and local barter currency, and implementing investment policies for their city, church, and union that reflect social responsibility criteria.

10. Promote fair trade not free trade

While we work to reform 'free trade' institutions and keep corporate chain stores out of our neighbourhoods, we should also promote our own vision of Fair Trade. We need to build networks of support and education for grassroots trade and trade in environmentally sustainable goods. We can promote labelling of goods such as Fair Trade Certified, organic, and sustainably harvested. We can purchase locally made goods and locally grown foods that support local economies and cooperative forms of production and trade.

■ The above information is from Global Exchange's website: www.globalexchange.org

© Global Exchange 2004

Brown promises to lead the world in cutting global debt

Britain wants the world to write off the debts of the poorest countries, sponsor new research into Aids vaccines and complete international trade talks next year

The Chancellor, who was setting out Britain's three main targets for its presidencies of G8 and the European Union, warned that it would be a 'make-or-break year' for development.

'We must, for the sake of the world's poorest, not squander but seize an opportunity to make a breakthrough on debt relief and development,' he said.

Mr Brown said he would press the United States to support both multilateral debt relief and his plan to double aid to the poorest countries.

He also called on all developed nations to declare a timetable for raising aid spending to 0.7 per cent of gross domestic product, as Britain has promised to do by 2013.

Aid agencies welcomed the Chancellor's pledge to put development at the forefront but said words needed to be backed by action.

Charles Bain, the director of Cafod, the Roman Catholic agency hosting the event in London at which the Chancellor spoke, called on him to ensure that other countries played their part.

By Jonathan Petre,
Religion Correspondent

'He must keep up the pressure on finance ministers, particularly in the US, to put global poverty at the top of their agenda,' said Mr Bain.

> *'We must, for the sake of the world's poorest, not squander but seize an opportunity to make a breakthrough on debt relief and development'*

Another agency, Oxfam, warned earlier this week that the failure of wealthy countries to meet promises first made five years ago will result in 45 million children dying in the next decade.

Mr Brown said that his plan for an International Finance Facility (IFF) would raise an extra $50 billion a year by issuing bonds using donors' long-term funding commitments as collateral.

The US has yet to endorse this, but in December 2004, Italy became the second G8 country to back the plan which Mr Brown says is needed if Millennium Development Goals of halving poverty and reducing infant mortality by two-thirds are to be met by 2015.

Alan Duncan, the Tory spokesman on international development, said: 'If Brown is serious about ending global poverty, he needs to explain exactly how he will take the lead in establishing freer and fairer trade, by his working through all the global institutions which have the power to shape it.

'Right on his doorstep is the EU, whose presidency we are about to hold, whose action, through its own protectionist practices, does so much to keep poor countries poor.'

■ Globalisation is an inevitable phenomenon in human history that's been bringing the world closer through the exchange of goods and products, information, knowledge and culture. (p. 1)

■ Supporters of globalisation say countries – like China, Vietnam, India and Uganda – that have opened up to the world economy have significantly reduced poverty. Critics argue that the process has exploited people in developing countries, caused massive disruptions and produced few benefits. (p. 1)

■ The accelerating pace of innovation in information technology (IT) is driving globalisation. The cost of a three-minute phone call from New York to London fell from $245 in 1930, to $3 in 1990, to about 35 cents in 1999 (1990 prices). (p. 4)

■ In the age of the internet, 1.3 billion people worldwide have to live on less than 70 pence a day, and 800 million people do not have enough to eat. (p. 5)

■ Trade allows people to buy goods and services that are not produced in their own countries. (p. 9)

■ International trade is a much more effective way to reduce poverty than outright aid because trade can help a country become self-sufficient, instead of relying on foreign aid. (p. 9)

■ Between 1980 and 1998, 19 of the world's 25 poorest countries experienced declining terms of trade. In both Nigeria and Uganda terms of trade fell by 70%. (p. 10)

■ Rich countries spend $1 billion a day on domestic agricultural subsidies – more than 6 times what they spend on overseas aid every year. Since 1997 these subsidies have increased by 25%. (p. 10)

■ While the developing world is struggling to attract trade, there is also a backlash against western workers as TNCs move their production plants abroad where wages will cost them so much less. (p. 13)

■ There is growing concern that globalisation is damaging the planet. Our environment continues to deteriorate, and many renewable resources such as fresh water, forests, plants and animal species are being exhausted beyond their natural recovery level. (p. 14)

■ The increased prosperity of globalisation goes hand-in-hand with mass poverty, and the widening of the gap between rich and poor. But well-managed and equitable growth has the potential to lift people out of poverty. (p. 16)

■ The average wage in a call centre is £12-15,000 ($19-23,500) compared with the per capita income of $24,160. Still, the 6,000 call centres in Britain employ nearly half a million people – 1.7% of the working population. (p. 19)

■ Worth around US$7 trillion each year, trade dominates the international agendas of most countries. (p. 21)

■ If UK consumption levels were matched globally, we would need eight planets to provide the resources needed. (p. 21)

■ Foreign investment has grown from $200m in 1990 to $884m in 1999. The UK is now the world's biggest foreign investor which means it has huge power over communities and workers around the world. (p. 25)

■ Transnational corporations (TNCs) such as Monsanto, Cargill, Nestlé and Wal-Mart have come to dominate supply chains for food and agricultural goods, from seed to supermarket shelf. (p. 28)

■ Two companies dominate sales of half the world's bananas, three trade 85% of the world's tea, and one, Wal-mart, now controls 40% of Mexico's retail food sector. It also found that Monsanto controls 91% of the global GM seed market. (p. 30)

■ Free trade means a country's economy is run without government intervention. It is a policy that rich country governments and international institutions are forcing poor countries to accept. (p. 31)

■ The International Labour Organisation's *World Employment* report said about 2.8 billion people were employed globally in 2003. But nearly 1.4 billion, the highest number ever, are living on less than $2 a day, while 550 million are living under the $1 poverty line. (p. 32)

■ Globalisation is more popular among the young. In France, 72% of those below 30 years of age say globalisation is a good thing, compared to 58% of respondents older than 50. More than 60% of young Peruvians view globalisation favourably, compared with only a third of those their parents' age. (p. 34)

■ Without fairer rules governing trade flows, immigration and labour standards, billions will continue to miss out on the rising global prosperity, prompting a fresh wave of international instability. (p. 36)

■ Women make up half the world but hold less than 5% of positions of power in determining global economic policy, and own an estimated 1% of global property. (p. 38)

ADDITIONAL RESOURCES

You might like to contact the following organisations for further information. Due to the increasing cost of postage, many organisations cannot respond to enquiries unless they receive a stamped, addressed envelope.

ActionAid
Hamlyn House
MacDonald Road
London, N19 5PG
Tel: 020 7561 7561
Fax: 020 7272 0899
E-mail: mail@actionaid.org.uk
Website: www.actionaid.org.uk
ActionAid's vision is a world without poverty in which every person can exercise their right to a life of dignity.

CAFOD – The Catholic Agency for Overseas Development
Romero Close
Stockwell Road
London, SW9 9TY
Tel: 020 7733 7900
Fax: 020 7274 9630
E-mail: hqcafod@cafod.org.uk
Website: www.cafod.org.uk
CAFOD is the development agency of the Catholic Church in England and Wales and works in partnership to tackle the causes of poverty regardless of race, religion or politics.

Christian Aid
35 Lower Marsh
Waterloo, London, SE1 7RT
Tel: 020 7620 4444
Fax: 020 7620 0719
E-mail: info@christian-aid.org
Website: www.christian-aid.org.uk
Christian Aid works in over 60 countries helping people, regardless of religion or race, to improve their own lives and tackle the causes of poverty and injustice.

Co-operative Group (CWS) Limited
New Century House
Manchester, M60 4ES
Tel: 0161 834 1212
E-mail: customer.relations@co-op.co.uk
Website: www.co-op.co.uk
The largest consumer co-op in the UK.

The Fairtrade Foundation
Suite 204
16 Baldwin's Gardens
London, EC1N 7RJ
Tel: 020 7405 5942
Fax: 020 7405 5943
E-mail: mail@fairtrade.org.uk
Website: www.fairtrade.org.uk
Works to ensure a better deal for marginalised and disadvantaged third world producers.

Friends of the Earth (FOE)
26-28 Underwood Street
London, N1 7JQ
Tel: 020 7490 1555
Fax: 020 7490 0881
E-mail: info@foe.co.uk
Website: www.foe.co.uk
As an independent environmental group, Friends of the Earth publishes a comprehensive range of leaflets, books and in-depth briefings and reports.

International Chamber of Commerce
75008 Paris, France
Tel: +33 1 49 53 28 28
Fax: +33 1 49 53 28 59
E-mail: icc@iccwbo.org
Website: www.iccwbo.org
ICC (International Chamber of Commerce) is the voice of world business championing the global economy as a force for economic growth, job creation and prosperity.

International Labour Organization (ILO)
Millbank Tower
21-24 Mill Bank
London, SW1P 4QP
Tel: 020 7828 6401
Fax: 020 7233 5925
E-mail: london@ilo.org
Website: www.ilo.org
The International Labour Organization is the United Nations agency with global responsibility for work, employment and labour market issues.

Oxfam
Oxfam House
274 Banbury Road
Oxford, OX2 7DZ
Tel: 01865 311311
Fax: 01865 312600
E-mail: oxfam@oxfam.org.uk
Website: www.oxfam.org.uk
Oxfam GB is a development, relief, and campaigning organisation dedicated to finding lasting solutions to poverty and suffering around the world.

Oxfam International Youth Parliament
PO Box 1711
Strawberry Hills 2012, NSW, Australia
Tel: +61 2 8204 3900
Fax: +61 2 8204 3426
E-mail: info@iyp.oxfam.org
Website: www.iyp.oxfam.org

People & Planet
51 Union Street
Oxford, OX4 1JP
Tel: 01865 245678
Fax: 01865 791927
E-mail: people@peopleandplanet.org
Website: www.peopleandplanet.org
Student action on poverty and the environment.

Save the Children
1 St John's Lane
London, EC1M 4AR
Tel: 020 7012 6400
Fax: 020 7012 6963
E-mail: enquiries@scfuk.org.uk
Website: www.savethechildren.org.uk
The leading UK charity working to create a better world for children.

The World Bank
1818 H Street, N.W.
Room U11-069
Washington, D.C. 20433, USA
Tel: + 1 202 473 1994
Fax: + 1 202 522 2422
E-mail: askus@worldbank.org
Website: www.worldbank.org
One of the world's largest sources of development assistance.

INDEX

ACKNOWLEDGEMENTS

The publisher is grateful for permission to reproduce the following material.

While every care has been taken to trace and acknowledge copyright, the publisher tenders its apology for any accidental infringement or where copyright has proved untraceable. The publisher would be pleased to come to a suitable arrangement in any such case with the rightful owner.

Overview
Globalisation, © The World Bank Group, Crack the code, © Save the Children, The rough guide to globalisation, © CAFOD, The IMF and World Bank, © New Internationalist, The IMF and World Bank – the statistics, © New Internationalist, Trade, © The World Bank Group, Free trade, © New Internationalist, Free trade statistics, © New Internationalist.

Chapter One: The Debate
Globalisation, © TheSite.org, The effects of globalisation, © Oxfam GB, Globalisation: a dirty word?, © Co-operative Group (CWS) Limited, Questions young people ask about globalisation, © Oxfam International Youth Parliament, British workers count the cost of globalisation, © Panos Features, Working poor, © International Labour Organization (ILO), What's wrong with world trade?,

© People & Planet, The stark reality of globalisation, © The National Kenyan Newspaper, The world for sale, © Friends of the Earth, Fairtrade retail sales, © The Fairtrade Foundation, Power hungry, © ActionAid International, Free trade leaves world food in grip of global giants, © Guardian Newspapers Limited 2005, Trade justice campaign, © Christian Aid, Half of all workers on $2 a day or less, © Guardian Newspapers Limited 2005, Analysing inequality, © International Chamber of Commerce, Living standards, © UNDP, How do people in different parts of the world view globalisation?, © International Chamber of Commerce, Poverty or prosperity, © 2005 Keith Porter, Labour market and economic indicators, © International Labour Office, World Employment Report 2004-2005, Global governance in crisis © Guardian Newspapers Limited 2005, 10 ways to democratise the global economy, © Global Exchange 2005, Brown promises to lead the world in cutting global debt, © Telegraph Group Limited, London 2005.

Photographs and illustrations:
Pages 1, 17, 39: Don Hatcher; pages 3, 22, 30, 37: Simon Kneebone; pages 5, 32: Angelo Madrid; pages 12, 25: Pumpkin House; pages 15, 28: Bev Aisbett.

Craig Donnellan
Cambridge
April, 2005